Easy knits for little ki

Easy knits
for little kids

CATHERINE TOUGH

PHOTOGRAPHS BY **John Heseltine**

C&T PUBLISHING

A Rowan publication

First published in North America by C&T Publishing Inc.,
PO Box 1456, Lafayette, CA 94549

Copyright © Rowan Yarns 2006
Design copyright © Catherine Tough 2006

Created by Berry & Co. (Publishing Ltd.) for Rowan Yarns

Project editor Susan Berry
US editor Sally Harding
Designer Anne Wilson
Stylist Susan Berry
Patterns Penny Hill, Sue Whiting

British Library Cataloguing in Publication Data
A catalog record for this book is available from the British Library.

ISBN-13: 978-1-57120-434-9
ISBN-10: 1-57120-434-2

Reproduced and printed in Malaysia

Contents

Introduction

Although I have been designing machine knitting for some years, I am not the world's greatest handknitter, so the patterns in this book are all for people like me—who like beautiful designs, but are a little lacking in handknitting skills or perhaps, more accurately, the time to practice!

In part the choices have been made to suit my own family's needs, which I feel are typical of many young working moms. I want something special for my daughter, hence the desire for the handknits, so that she can keep some of them when she is older and remind herself of the fun she had in them.

My husband, Ras, comes from Trinidad, so we occasionally go on long-haul flights. With a fractious child in tow, you need all the creature comforts you can get. This led to my creation of the pillows, robe, comfy socks, and slippers—all ideal for nighttime traveling! The big Fred doll is perhaps a trifle large for hand baggage— sorry about that.

I do hope this book inspires you to take up knitting or, if you can knit already, knit some more!

I have arranged the patterns into two chapters:

ON THE GO

This has some great knits for kids who are out and about, including cute retro-style balaclavas in singing colors, matching scarves, mittens, and wristwarmers to keep cozy when playing outside, handy bags for those essential little odds and ends, a really versatile little garter stitch jacket, a pretty as a picture pinafore dress, an easy wrap-around skirt, plus a pair of eye-catching sweaters with animal motifs. What more could a little kid want?

COMFORT ZONE

These designs are for those times when your children want to be cozy and comforted, with some lovely soft yarns. This is your chance to show how much you care, by creating some great handknits for the nursery, too. I have even included a knitted sleepover mat. Well, it is so easy you might get around to it, and if you make it, you will look like a super-caring mom in front of all his or her friends!

Anyway, I hope you have as much fun knitting these things as I did designing them and my daughter, Abi, and her friend, Jayden, did modeling them for you.

Catherine Tough

ON THE GO

Swing coat

This little coat or jacket is just amazingly versatile, because it looks beautiful over a pretty dress for best, but is also really comfortable for messing around in the playground over a T-shirt and pair of jeans, as my daughter, Abi, demonstrates here. Getting her into a dress at all would have been hard to demonstrate at the moment becasue she has strong views about what she likes to wear.

Knitted in garter stitch, the swing coat, with its slightly flaring line, is inspired by some of the designs of the 1940s. If you want your daughter to wear it over a thick sweater in winter time, knit it in a bigger size.

The yarn, Rowan's *Baby Alpaca*, is a bit of a treat because not only does it feel wonderfully soft to the touch, it is elastic and strong, giving the garment great shape. I think this one is a classic, and will be passed on to one of Abi's cousins or friends when she grows out of it.

Which sizes?

To fit ages

| 3–4 | 4–5 | 5–6 | years |

FINISHED MEASUREMENTS

Around chest

| 27½ | 29½ | 31½ | in |
| 70 | 75 | 80 | cm |

Length from shoulder

| 12½ | 14 | 15¾ | in |
| 32 | 36 | 40 | cm |

Sleeve seam

| 9¾ | 11 | 12¼ | in |
| 25 | 28 | 31 | cm |

Which yarns?

6 (7: 8) x 50g/1¾oz balls of Rowan *RYC Baby Alpaca DK* in Chambray 201

Which needles?

Pair of size 5 (3¾mm) knitting needles

What extras?

1 button

What gauge?

22 sts and 40 rows to 4in/10cm measured over garter st using size 5 (3¾mm) needles *or size to obtain correct gauge*.

Abbreviations?

See page 125.

Back

Using size 5 (3.75mm) needles, cast on 97 (105: 113) sts. Work in garter st (K every row) for 5 (9: 13) rows, ending with RS facing for next row.

Next row (RS) K6, skp, K to last 8 sts, K2tog, K6.

Work 7 rows.

Rep last 8 rows 7 (8: 9) times more, then first of these rows (the dec row) again. 79 (85: 91) sts.

Work even until Back measures 7½ (8½: 9¾)in/19 (22: 25)cm, ending with RS facing for next row.

SHAPE ARMHOLES

Bind off 5 (6: 7) sts at beg of next 2 rows. 69 (73: 77) sts.

Next row (RS) K2, skp, K to last 4 sts, K2tog, K2.

Working all armhole decreases as set by last row, dec 1 st at each end of 2nd and foll 3 alt rows. 59 (63: 67) sts.

Work even until armhole measures 5 (5½: 6)in/13 (14: 15)cm, ending with RS facing for next row.

SHAPE SHOULDERS

Bind off 9 (9: 10) sts at beg of next 2 rows, then 9 (10: 10) sts at beg of foll 2 rows.

Bind off rem 23 (25: 27) sts.

Left front

Using size 5 (3.75mm) needles, cast on 44 (47: 50) sts. Work in garter st for 5 (9: 13) rows, ending with RS facing for next row.

Next row (RS) K6, skp, K to last 6 sts, M1, K6.

Work 7 rows.

Rep last 8 rows 7 (8: 9) times more, then first of these rows (the shaping row) again. 44 (47: 50) sts.

Work even until Left Front matches Back to start of armhole shaping, ending with RS facing for next row.

SHAPE ARMHOLE

Bind off 5 (6: 7) sts at beg of next 2 rows. 39 (41: 43) sts.

Work 1 row.

Working all armhole decreases as set by Back, dec 1 st at armhole edge of next and foll 4 alt rows. 34 (36: 38) sts.

Work even until Left Front matches Back to start of shoulder shaping, ending with RS facing for next row.

SHAPE SHOULDER

Bind off 9 (9: 10) sts at beg of next row, then 9 (10: 10) sts at beg of foll alt row, ending with **WS** facing for next row. 16 (17: 18) sts.

SHAPE COLLAR

Row 1 (RS of collar) K9 (9: 10) and turn.

Rows 2 to 6 Knit.

Rep last 6 rows until shorter row-end edge of collar extension fits across to center back neck.

Bind off.

Right front

Using size 5 (3.75mm) needles, cast on 44 (47: 50) sts.

Work in garter st for 5 (9: 13) rows, ending with RS facing for next row.

Next row (RS) K6, M1, K to last 8 sts, K2tog, K6.

Work 7 rows.

Rep last 8 rows 7 (8: 9) times more, then first of these rows (the shaping row) again. 44 (47: 50) sts.

Work even until Right Front matches Back to start of armhole shaping, ending with **WS** facing for next row.

SHAPE ARMHOLE

Bind off 5 (6: 7) sts at beg of next 2 rows. 39 (41: 43) sts.

Working all armhole decreases as set by Back, dec 1 st at armhole edge of next and foll 4 alt rows. 34 (36: 38) sts.

Work 1 row, ending with RS facing for next row.

Next row (RS) K4, K2tog, [yo] twice (to make a buttonhole), skp, K to end.

Next row K to end, working twice into double yo of previous row.

Work even until Right Front matches Back to start of shoulder shaping, ending with **WS** facing for next row.

SHAPE SHOULDER

Bind off 9 (9: 10) sts at beg of next row, then 9 (10: 10) sts at beg of foll alt row, ending with RS facing for next row. 16 (17: 18) sts.

SHAPE COLLAR

Row 1 (WS of collar) K9 (9: 10) and turn.

Rows 2 to 6 Knit.

Rep last 6 rows until shorter row-end edge of collar extension fits across to center back neck.

Bind off.

Sleeves

Using size 5 (3.75mm) needles, cast on 39 (43: 47) sts.

Work in garter st for 21 rows, ending with RS facing for next row.

Next row (RS) K4, M1, K to last 4 sts, M1, K4. 41 (45: 49) sts.

Working all increases as set by last row, inc 1 st at each end of 8th and every foll 8th row until there are 57 (63: 67) sts.

Work even until Sleeve measures 9¾ (11: 12¼)in/ 25 (28: 31)cm, ending with RS facing for next row.

SHAPE TOP OF SLEEVE

Bind off 5 (6: 7) sts at beg of next 2 rows. 47 (51: 53) sts.

Next row (RS) K2, skp, K to last 4 sts, K2tog, K2.

Next row Knit.

Rep last 2 rows 4 times more.

Bind off rem 37 (41: 43) sts.

Finishing

Do NOT press.

Sew shoulder seams. Sew together bound-off edges of collar extensions, then sew shorter row-end edge to back neck. Sew side seams. Sew sleeve seams. Sew Sleeves into armholes. Sew on button.

Balaclavas

This is another retro design, which is worth recycling because it is so practical. Not only is it warm and covers cold ears in winter, but it is hard to pull off or lose! The fact that Abi and Jayden were happy enough to play wearing them proves the point.

I made two colorways, a unisex one in two shades of green and a really girlie one in pink (currently Abi's favorite color).

They mix and match with the scarves, mittens, and wristwarmers featured in this chapter.

The balaclavas are quite stretchy so they come in just two sizes: one should fit most 3 to 4 year olds, and the bigger one the 5 to 6 year olds.

Which sizes?

To fit ages 3–4 (5–6) years

Which yarns?

BOY'S BALACLAVA

1 x 50g/1¾oz ball of Jaeger *Matchmaker Merino DK* in each of **MC** (Loden 730) and **CC** (Mushroom 880)

GIRL'S BALACLAVA

1 x 50g/1¾oz ball of Jaeger *Matchmaker Merino DK* in each of **MC** (Petal 883) and **CC** (Rock Rose 896)

Which needles?

Pair of size 3 (3.25mm) knitting needles

Pair of size 6 (4mm) knitting needles

What gauge?

22 sts and 30 rows to 4in/10cm over st st using size 6 (4mm) needles *or size to obtain correct gauge.*

Abbreviations?

See page 125.

Balaclava

Using size 3 (3.25mm) needles and CC, cast on 88 (96) sts.

Row 1 (RS) *K1, P1, rep from * to end.

Row 2 As row 1.

These 2 rows form rib.

Work in rib for 14 (18) rows more, ending with RS facing for next row.

Set aside this ball of CC—it will be used for Front Edging.

Slip first and last 12 (14) sts onto holders, leaving 64 (68) sts at center.

With RS facing, using size 6 (4mm) needles and MC, rejoin yarn to center sts and work in patt as foll:

Rows 1 and 2 Knit.

Row 3 (RS) Knit.

Row 4 Purl.

Rows 5 to 10 As rows 3 and 4, 3 times.

These 10 rows form patt.

Work in patt until Balaclava measures approximately 8½ (9¾)in/22 (25)cm from cast-on edge, ending after patt row 3 and with **WS** facing for next row.

SHAPE TOP

Row 1 (WS) Patt 43 (47) sts, P2tog and turn.

Row 2 Sl 1, patt 22 (26) sts, skp and turn.

Row 3 Sl 1, patt 22 (26) sts, P3tog and turn.

Row 4 Sl 1, patt 22 (26) sts, sK2p and turn.

Row 5 Sl 1, patt 22 (26) sts, P2tog and turn.

Rep rows 2 to 5, 5 times more, then rows 2 and 3 again.

Break off yarn and leave rem 24 (28) sts on another holder.

Finishing

Press lightly following instructions on yarn label.

FRONT EDGING

With RS facing, using size 3 (3.25mm) needles and ball of CC set to one side, rib across first set of 12 (14) sts left on a holder, pick up and knit 44 (51) sts up first side of face opening, knit across 24 (28) sts left on last holder, pick up and knit 44 (51) sts down second side of face opening, then rib across last set of 12 (14) sts left on a holder. 136 (158) sts.

Work in rib as set for 7 rows more, ending with RS facing for next row.

Bind off in rib.

Sew front seam.

His and hers bags

How big?
The finished bag measures 8½in/22cm wide and 10½in/27cm deep.

Which yarns?
BOY'S BAG
2 x 50g/1¾oz balls of Rowan *Cotton Rope* in **MC** (Harbour 068) and 1 ball in **CC** (Calypso 064)
GIRL'S BAG
2 x 50g/1¾oz balls of Rowan Cotton Rope in **MC** (Cyclamen 071) and 1 ball in **CC** (Fruit Gum 062)

Which needles?
Pair of size 9 (5.5mm) knitting needles

What gauge?
16 sts and 22 rows to 4in/10cm measured over st st using size 9 (5.5mm) needles *or size to obtain correct gauge.*

Abbreviations?
See page 125.

If you are looking for an easy project having just learned to knit, you can't go far wrong with this simple drawstring bag, which is designed in garter stitch and stockinette stitch, the first stitches you learn, and a pretty basic colorway change. It shouldn't take you too long to make, even if you are a really new knitter.

I designed the bag so that it can be worn either over the shoulder, as the kids demonstrate here, or across the back with the arms going through the two loops. It is a handy size for storing a small toy or two and a few personal odds and ends.

It wouldn't be too hard to make a bigger one for yourself; just allow a few more stitches and a little more yarn.

Bag

Using size 9 (5.5mm) needles and MC, cast on 71 sts.
Work in garter st (K every row) for 11 rows, ending with RS facing for next row.
Join in CC.
Using CC, work in garter st for 10 rows.
Using MC, work in garter st for 10 rows.
Using CC, work in garter st for 10 rows.
Break off CC and cont using MC only.
Starting with a K row, work in st st until Bag measures 9½in/24cm, ending with RS facing for next row.
Next row (eyelet row) (RS) K5, *yo, K2tog, K10, rep from * to last 6 sts, yo, K2tog, K4.
Work in garter st for 8 rows, ending with **WS** facing for next row.
Bind off knitwise (on **WS**).

Drawstring

Using size 9 (5.5mm) needles and CC, cast on 160 sts.
Bind off knitwise.

Finishing

Press lightly following instructions on yarn label.
Fold Bag in half and sew side and base seam. Starting and ending at side seam, thread Drawstring through eyelet row and knot ends together.

Pompom hats

Just great for a first-time knitter as they are so quick and easy to knit, these pompom hats can be fun to make with your children—they will enjoy helping you wind the yarn around the cardboard when you make the pompoms. I chose to make the pompoms in the contrasting colors, but you could make two-tone versions or even a few giant multicolored ones for the kids to play with as well.

I made a girl's and a boy's version of the hat here to go with the sweaters, scarves, and mittens, but as they take very little yarn, you can use leftovers from any other knitting projects on the go if you prefer.

Which sizes?
To fit ages 3–6 years
Note: The finished hat measures 20in/51cm around head.

Which yarns?
BOY'S BAG
1 x 50g/1¾oz ball of Jaeger *Matchmaker Merino DK* in each of **MC** (Flannel 782) and **CC** (Sage 857)
GIRL'S BAG
1 x 50g/1¾oz ball of Jaeger *Matchmaker Merino DK* in each of **MC** (Petal 883) and **CC** (Rock Rose 896)

Which needles?
Pair of size 3 (3.25mm) knitting needles
Pair of size 6 (4mm) knitting needles

What gauge?
22 sts and 40 rows to 4in/10cm measured over seed st using size 6 (4mm) needles *or size to obtain correct gauge.*

Abbreviations?
See page 125.

Hat
Using size 6 (4mm) needles and CC, cast on 110 sts.
Break off CC and join in MC.
Row 1 (WS of turn-back, RS of Hat) P2, *K2, P2, rep from * to end.
Row 2 K2, *P2, K2, rep from * to end.
These 2 rows form rib.
Work in rib for 14 rows more, ending with RS facing for next row.
Change to size 3 (3.25mm) needles.
Work in rib for 16 rows more, inc 1 st at each end of last row and ending with RS of Hat (**WS** of turn-back) facing for next row. 112 sts.
Change to size 6 (4mm) needles.

Now work in seed st as foll:

Row 1 (RS of Hat) *K1, P1, rep from * to end.

Row 2 *P1, K1, rep from * to end.

These 2 rows form seed st.

Work in seed st for 22 rows more, ending with RS facing for next row.

SHAPE CROWN

Row 1 (RS) Seed st 5 sts, work 3 tog, [seed st 8 sts, work 3 tog] 9 times, seed st to end. 92 sts.

Work 3 rows.

Row 5 Seed st 4 sts, work 3 tog, [seed st 6 sts, work 3 tog] 9 times, seed st to end. 72 sts.

Work 3 rows.

Row 9 Seed st 3 sts, work 3 tog, [seed st 4 sts, work 3 tog] 9 times, seed st to end. 52 sts.

Work 3 rows.

Row 13 [Seed st 2 sts, work 3 tog] 10 times, seed st to end. 32 sts.

Work 3 rows.

Row 17 Seed st 1 st, [work 3 tog] 10 times, seed st 1 st.

Break off yarn and thread through rem 12 sts. Pull up tight and fasten off securely.

Finishing

Press lightly following instructions on yarn label.

Sew back seam, reversing seam for turn-back.

Using CC, make a 2in/5cm diameter pompom and attach to top of Hat.

Striped scarves

This is one of the easiest projects in the book, and comes in two versions, one for a boy and one for a girl. I have designed the scarves to go with the pompom hats, balaclavas, mittens, or wristwarmers, so your child can have a great mix and match outfit in either masculine grays and greens or girlie pinks.

I like the current fashion for narrow scarves. These are long so they can be wrapped around a few times on cold days, but it would be easy, if you wanted to, to make the scarves wider and shorter, simply by adding a few more stitches when you cast on, and stopping knitting when you have reached the end of a stripe repeat.

How big?

The finished scarf measures 4in/10cm wide and 38½in/98cm long.

Which yarns?

BOY'S SCARF

1 x 50g/1¾oz ball of Jaeger *Matchmaker Merino DK* in each of **MC** (Flannel 782), **A** (Sage 857), **B** (Pumpkin 898), **C** (Mushroom 880), and **D** (Teal 790)

GIRL'S SCARF

1 x 50g/1¾oz ball of Jaeger *Matchmaker Merino DK* in each of **MC** (Petal 883), **A** (Rock Rose 896), **B** (Marine 914), **C** (Flannel 782), and **D** (Sage 857)

Which needles?

Pair of size 6 (4mm) knitting needles

What gauge?

22 sts and 30 rows to 4in/10cm measured over st st using size 6 (4mm) needles *or size to obtain correct gauge.*

Abbreviations?

See page 125.

Scarf

Using size 6 (4mm) needles and MC, cast on 23 sts.

Work in garter st (K every row) for 4 rows, ending with RS facing for next row.

Joining in and breaking off colors as required, now work in patt as foll:

Row 1 (RS) Using MC, knit.

Row 2 Using MC, K3, P17, K3.

Rows 3 to 10 As rows 1 and 2, 4 times.

Row 11 Using A, knit.

Row 12 Using A, K3, P17, K3.

Rows 13 to 22 As rows 1 and 2, 5 times.

Row 23 Using B, knit.

Row 24 Using B, K3, P17, K3.

Rows 25 to 34 As rows 1 and 2, 5 times.

Row 35 Using C, knit.

Row 36 Using C, K3, P17, K3.

Rows 37 to 46 As rows 1 and 2, 5 times.

Row 47 Using D, knit.

Row 48 Using D, K3, P17, K3.

These 48 rows form patt.

Rep last 48 rows 4 times more, then rows 1 to 46 again, ending after 10 rows using MC and with RS facing for next row.

Using MC, work in garter st for 5 rows, ending with **WS** facing for next row.

Bind off knitwise (on **WS**).

Finishing

Press lightly following instructions on yarn label.

Wristwarmers

These little wristwarmers are designed to go with the other accessories in this book. They come in two versions, a girl's and a boy's, with a very slight difference in the design of each, as well as in the usual colorways. The boy's version is striped whereas the girl's version is a self-colored textured stripe, tipped at each end with another color.

I find children often prefer wearing fingerless gloves because they don't have to keep taking them on and off. I have made the hand part quite long to keep the fingers as warm as possible, but if you find they are too long for you child, just knit a few less rows when you get to this part of the pattern.

Which sizes?
The finished boy's and girl's wristwarmers measure 6¼ (7)in/ 16 (18)cm around palm of hand.

Which yarns?
BOY'S WRISTWARMERS
1 x 50g/1¾oz ball of Jaeger *Matchmaker Merino DK* in each of **A** (Loden 730), **B** (Mushroom 880), **C** (Sage 857), and **D** (Teal 790)
GIRL'S WRISTWARMERS
1 x 50g/1¾oz ball of Jaeger *Matchmaker Merino DK* in each of **MC** (Petal 883) and **CC** (Rock Rose 896)

Which needles?
Pair of size 6 (4mm) knitting needles

What gauge?
22 sts and 40 rows to 4in/10cm measured over seed st using size 6 (4mm) needles *or size to obtain correct gauge.*

Abbreviations?
See page 125.

BOY'S WRISTWARMERS (both alike)

Using size 6 (4mm) needles and A, cast on
35 (39) sts.
Row 1 (WS) Knit.
Break off A and join in B.
Now work in seed st as foll:
Row 1 (RS) K1, *P1, K1, rep from * to end.
Row 2 As row 1.
These 2 rows form seed st.
Work in seed st for 5 (6) rows more, ending with
WS (RS) facing for next row.
Join in C.
Using C, work in seed st for 7 (8) rows.
Join in D.
Using D, work in seed st for 1 row more, ending
with **WS** facing for next row.
SHAPE THUMB OPENING
Next row (WS) Using D, seed st 16 (18) sts, bind
off 3 sts in seed st, seed st to end.
Next row Using D, seed st 16 (18) sts, turn
and cast on 9 (11) sts, turn and seed st to end.
41 (47) sts.
Using D, work 2 rows.
Next row (WS) Using D, seed st 19 (22) sts,
work 3 tog, seed st to end. 39 (45) sts.
Using D, work 1 (2) rows.
Using B, work 2 rows.
Next row Using B, seed st 18 (21) sts, work
3 tog, seed st to end. 37 (43) sts.
Using B, work 3 (4) rows.
Next row Using B, seed st 17 (20) sts, work
3 tog, seed st to end. 35 (41) sts.
Using C, work 3 (4) rows.
Next row Using C, seed st 16 (19) sts, work
3 tog, seed st to end. 33 (39) sts.

Using C, work 3 rows.

Using D, work 7 (8) rows.

Using B, work 7 (8) rows.

Using C, work 7 (8) rows.

Using D, work 7 rows, ending with **WS** facing for next row.

Break off B, C, and D and join in A.

Next row (WS) Purl.

Rep last row once more.

Bind off purlwise (on **WS**).

Finishing

Press lightly following instructions on yarn label.

Sew side seam.

GIRL'S WRISTWARMERS (both alike)

Using size 6 (4mm) needles and CC, cast on 35 (39) sts.

Row 1 (WS) Knit.

Break off CC and join in MC.

Now work in patt as foll:

Row 1 (RS) Knit.

Row 2 Purl.

Rows 3 to 6 As rows 1 and 2, twice.

Rows 7 and 8 Knit.

These 8 rows form patt.

Work in patt for 8 rows more, ending with RS facing for next row.

SHAPE THUMB OPENING

Next row (RS) K16 (18), bind off 3 sts, K to end.

Next row P16 (18), turn and cast on 9 (11) sts, turn and P to end. 41 (47) sts.

Work 2 rows.

Next row (RS) K17 (20), K2tog, K3, skp, K to end. 39 (45) sts.

Work 3 rows.

Next row (RS) K16 (19), K2tog, K3, skp, K to end. 37 (43) sts.

Work 3 rows.

Next row (RS) K15 (18), K2tog, K3, skp, K to end. 35 (41) sts.

Work 3 rows.

Next row (RS) K14 (17), K2tog, K3, skp, K to end. 33 (39) sts.

Work even in patt until Wristwarmer measures approximately 6¼ (7)in/16 (18)cm from cast-on edge, ending after patt row 6 and with RS facing for next row.

Break off MC and join in CC.

Next row (RS) Knit.

Rep last row once more.

Bind off.

Finishing

Press lightly following instructions on yarn label.

Sew side seam.

Animal picture sweaters

I thought it might be fun to make two different versions of the same sweater, one with a rabbit and the other with a frog on the front, and I chose colorways that went well with these images—well, frogs are greenish anyway, and rabbits are quite pretty so pink didn't seem a bad idea—but it is entirely your own choice what you put on the front of which, preferably in a matching or toning color.

The pattern that follows is for the two versions of the sweaters. The two different motif patterns are given last so that you can choose the animal you like best. The appliqué is made from a simple piece of felted knitting, which is cut into shape and stitched to the front of the sweater.

Which sizes?

To fit ages

3–4	4–5	5–6	years

FINISHED MEASUREMENTS

Around chest

25½	27½	29½	in
65	70	75	cm

Length from shoulder

13¼	14½	15¾	in
34	37	40	cm

Sleeve seam

9¾	11	12¼	in
25	28	31	cm

Which yarns?

STRIPED SWEATER

2 (2: 3) x 50g/1¾oz balls of Rowan *RYC Cashsoft DK* in **MC** (Bloom 520), and 1 (1: 2) balls in each of **A** (Poppy 512) and **B** (Clementine 510)

COLOR BLOCK SWEATER

3 (3: 4) x 50g/1¾oz balls of Rowan *RYC Cashsoft DK* in **MC** (Tape 515), 1 (1: 2) balls in **A** (Sage 516), and 2 (2: 3) balls in **B** (Lime 509)

RABBIT APPLIQUÉ

1 x 50g/1¾oz ball of Rowan *Scottish Tweed DK* in Porridge 024

FROG APPLIQUÉ

1 x 50g/1¾oz ball of Rowan *Scottish Tweed DK* in Celtic Mix 022

Which needles?

Pair of size 5 (3.75mm) knitting needles
Pair of size 6 (4mm) knitting needles

What extras?

FOR APPLIQUÉS

Buttons—2 for frog, or 1 for rabbit
Matching sewing thread
For rabbit, scrap of brown yarn for nose, and black sewing thread for mouth

What gauge?

22 sts and 30 rows to 4in/10cm measured over st st using size 6 (4mm) needles *or size to obtain correct gauge.*

Abbreviations?

See page 125.

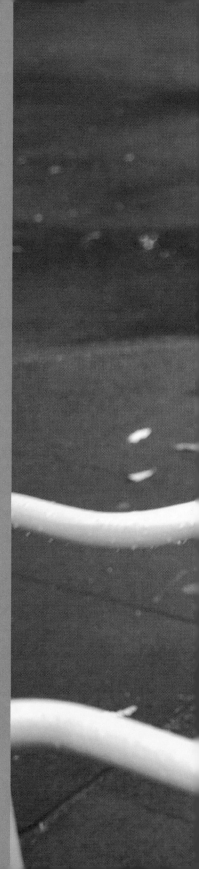

STRIPED SWEATER

Back

Using size 5 (3.75mm) needles and A, cast on 74 (78: 86) sts.

Row 1 (RS) K2, *P2, K2, rep from * to end.

Row 2 P2, *K2, P2, rep from * to end.

These 2 rows form rib.

Work in rib for 16 rows more, inc 0 (1: 0) st at each end of last row and ending with RS facing for next row. 74 (80: 86) sts.

Break off A and join in MC.

Change to size 6 (4mm) needles.**

Starting with a K row, work in striped st st as foll:

Using MC, work 10 rows.

Join in B.

Using B, work 10 rows.

These 20 rows form striped st st.

Work even in striped st st until Back measures 8¼ (9: 9¾)in/21 (23: 25)cm, ending with RS facing for next row.

SHAPE ARMHOLES

Keeping stripes correct, bind off 5 (6: 7) sts at beg of next 2 rows. 64 (68: 72) sts.

Work even until armhole measures 4¼ (4¾: 5)in/11 (12: 13)cm, ending with RS facing for next row.

SHAPE BACK NECK

Next row (RS) K21 (22: 23) and turn, leaving rem sts on a holder.

Work each side of neck separately.

Dec 1 st at neck edge of next 3 rows, ending with RS facing for next row. 18 (19: 20) sts.

Work 2 rows, ending with RS facing for next row.

SHAPE SHOULDER

Bind off.

With RS facing, slip center 22 (24: 26) sts onto a holder, rejoin appropriate yarn to rem sts, K to end.

Complete to match first side, reversing shapings.

Front

Work as given for Back until 12 rows less have been worked than on Back to start of back neck shaping, ending with RS facing for next row.

SHAPE FRONT NECK

Next row (RS) K26 (27: 28) and turn, leaving rem sts on a holder.

Work each side of neck separately.

Dec 1 st at neck edge of next 8 rows, ending with **WS** facing for next row. 18 (19: 20) sts.

Work 9 rows, ending with RS facing for next row.

SHAPE SHOULDER

Bind off.

With RS facing, slip center 12 (14: 16) sts onto a holder, rejoin appropriate yarn to rem sts, K to end.

Complete to match first side, reversing shapings.

Sleeves

Using size 5 (3.75mm) needles and A, cast on 38 (42: 46) sts.

Work in rib as given for Back for 16 rows, ending with RS facing for next row.

Change to size 6 (4mm) needles.

Break off A and join in MC.

Starting with a K row, work in st st, shaping sides by inc 1 st at each end of 3rd (5th: 7th) and every foll 6th row until there are 56 (62: 66) sts.

Work even until Sleeve measures 9¾ (11: 12¼)in/25 (28: 31)cm, ending with RS facing for next row.

SHAPE TOP OF SLEEVE

Mark both ends of last row to denote top of sleeve seam.

Work 6 (8: 10) rows more, ending with RS facing for next row.

Bind off.

Finishing

Press lightly on **WS** following instructions on yarn label and avoiding ribbing.

Sew right shoulder seam.

NECKBAND

With RS facing, using size 5 (3.75mm) needles and A, pick up and knit 16 sts down left side of front neck, K across 12 (14: 16) sts on Front holder, pick up and knit 16 sts up right side of front neck, and 6 sts down right side of back neck, K across 22 (24: 26) sts on Back holder, then pick up and knit 6 sts up left side of back neck. 78 (82: 86) sts.

Starting with row 2, work in rib as given for Back for 5 rows, ending with RS of body facing for next row.

Bind off in rib.

Sew left shoulder and Neckband seam. Matching sleeve markers to top of side seams and center of sleeve bound-off edge, sew Sleeves into armholes. Sew side and sleeve seams.

COLOR BLOCK SWEATER

Back

Work as given for Back of Striped Sweater to **.

Starting with a K row, work in st st using MC only and complete as given for Back of Striped Sweater.

Front

Work as given for Front of Striped Sweater, noting that st st section is worked using MC only.

Sleeves

Work as given for Sleeves of Striped Sweater, but using B in place of MC.

Finishing

Press lightly on **WS** following instructions on yarn label and avoiding ribbing.

Sew right shoulder seam.

NECKBAND

Work as given for Neckband of Striped Sweater.

Sew left shoulder and Neckband seam. Matching sleeve markers to top of side seams and center of sleeve bound-off edge, sew Sleeves into armholes. Sew side and sleeve seams.

APPLIQUÉ

Rabbit appliqué

Using size 6 (4mm) needles, cast on 50 sts.

Starting with a K row, work in st st for 6¼in/16cm.

Bind off.

Machine hot wash and tumble dry knitted piece to shrink and felt it. Press felted piece. Using Rabbit template (see page 124), cut out rabbit shape and overcast stitch to Front of Sweater. Using photograph as a guide, sew on button to form eye. Embroider nose using scrap of brown yarn and satin stitch, then embroider backstitch mouth using sewing thread.

Frog appliqué

Using size 6 (4mm) needles, cast on 60 sts.

Starting with a K row, work in st st for 7in/18cm.

Bind off.

Machine hot wash and tumble dry knitted piece to shrink and felt it. Press felted piece. Using Frog template (see page 124), cut out frog shape and overcast stitch to Front of Sweater. Using photograph as a guide, sew on buttons to form eyes.

Pinafore dress

This little knitted dress is so comfortable to wear that I couldn't persuade Abi to take it off! With a ribbed yoke and stockinette stitch skirt, it is really easy to knit as well, because it has only minimal shaping and no sleeves to deal with. The little pocket makes a pretty detail—just one pocket is placed on the right-hand side at hip level, but you could knit two if you wish.

The contrasting edging around the sleeves and neckline, and on the pocket, is a nice finishing touch, as is the little heart on the pocket.

You can combine the dress with the hat and any of the scarves for a matching set to complete the outfit.

Which sizes?

To fit ages

3–4	4–5	5–6	years

FINISHED MEASUREMENTS

Around chest

23½	25½	27½	in
60	65	70	cm

Length from shoulder

22¾	24¾	26¾	in
58	63	68	cm

Which yarns?

6 (7: 8) x 50g/1¾oz balls of Jaeger *Extra Fine Merino Chunky* in **MC** (Alaska 011)

1 x 50g/1¾oz ball of Jaeger *Matchmaker Merino DK* in **CC** (Rosy 870)

Which needles?

Pair of size 9 (5.5mm) knitting needles

Pair of size 10 (6mm) knitting needles

What extras?

2 buttons

What gauge?

15 sts and 20 rows to 4in/10cm measured over st st using size 10 (6mm) needles and **MC** *or size to obtain correct gauge.*

Abbreviations?

See page 125.

Back

Using size 9 (5.5mm) needles and CC DOUBLE, cast on 57 (61: 65) sts.

Row 1 (WS) Knit.

Break off CC and join in MC.

Rows 2 and 3 Knit.

Change to size 10 (6mm) needles.

Starting with a K row, work in st st for 6 (10: 14) rows, ending with RS facing for next row.

Next row (RS) K6 (7: 8), skp, K to last 8 (9: 10) sts, K2tog, K to end.

Working all side seam decreases as set by last row, dec 1 st at each end of 12th and every foll 12th row until 45 (49: 53) sts rem.

Work even until Back measures 15 (16: 17¼)in/38 (41: 44)cm, ending with RS facing for next row.**

Next row (RS) K1, *P1, K1, rep from * to end.

Next row P1, *K1, P1, rep from * to end.

These 2 rows form rib.

Work in rib until Back measures 18 (20½: 22)in/46 (52: 56)cm, ending with RS facing for next row.

SHAPE ARMHOLES

Bind off 4 sts at beg of next 2 rows. 37 (41: 45) sts.

Dec 1 st at each end of next 3 rows. 31 (35: 39) sts.

Work even until armhole measures 4 (3½: 4)in/ 10 (9: 10)cm, ending with RS facing for next row.

SHAPE BACK NECK AND SHOULDER STRAPS

Next row (RS) Rib 8 (9: 10) and turn, leaving rem sts on a holder.

Work each side of neck separately.

Dec 1 st at neck edge of next row, ending with RS facing for next row. 7 (8: 9) sts.

Work 2 rows, ending with RS facing for next row.

Mark both ends of last row to denote shoulder line.

Work 6 rows more, ending with RS facing for next row.

Work in garter st (K each row) for 2 rows.

Bind off.

With RS facing, rejoin yarn to rem sts, bind off center 15 (17: 19) sts, rib to end.

Complete to match first side, reversing shapings.

Front

Work as given for Back to **.

Next row (RS) P1, *K1, P1, rep from * to end.

Next row K1, *P1, K1, rep from * to end.

These 2 rows form rib.

Work in rib until Front matches Back to start of armhole shaping, ending with RS facing for next row.

SHAPE ARMHOLES

Bind off 4 sts at beg of next 2 rows. 37 (41: 45) sts.

Dec 1 st at each end of next 4 rows. 29 (33: 37) sts.

Work 4 rows, ending with RS facing for next row.

SHAPE FRONT NECK AND SHOULDER STRAPS

Next row (RS) Rib 10 (11: 12) and turn, leaving rem sts on a holder.

Work each side of neck separately.

Dec 1 st at neck edge of next 3 rows, ending with RS facing for next row. 7 (8: 9) sts.

Work even until 4 rows less have been worked than on Back to shoulder line, ending with RS facing for next row.

Next row (RS) Rib 2 (2: 3), work 2 tog, yo (to make a buttonhole), rib 3 (4: 4).

Work 3 rows more, ending with RS facing for next row.

Work in garter st (K each row) for 2 rows.

Bind off.

With RS facing, rejoin yarn to rem sts, bind off center 9 (11: 13) sts, rib to end.

Complete to match first side, reversing shapings and working buttonhole row as foll:

Next row (RS) Rib 3 (4: 4), yo (to make a buttonhole), work 2 tog, rib 2 (2: 3).

Pocket

Using size 10 (6mm) needles and MC, cast on 12 sts.

Starting with a K row, work in st st for 16 rows, ending with RS facing for next row.

Change to size 9 (5.5mm) needles.

Work in garter st (K each row) for 2 rows.

Break off M and join in CC DOUBLE.

Work in garter st for 2 rows more, ending with RS facing for next row.

Bind off.

Finishing

Press lightly on **WS** following instructions on yarn label.
Sew side seams.

ARMHOLE BORDERS (both alike)

With RS facing, using size 9 (5.5mm) needles and MC, pick up and knit 57 (61: 65) sts evenly all round armhole edge.

***Row 1 (WS) Knit.

Break off MC and join in CC DOUBLE.

Work in garter st (K each row) for 2 rows, ending with RS facing for next row.

Bind off.

BACK NECKBAND

With RS facing, using size 9 (5.5mm) needles and MC, pick up and knit 8 sts down right side of back neck, 15 (17: 19) sts from Back, then 8 sts up left side of back neck. 31 (33: 35) sts.

Complete as given for Armhole Borders from ***.

FRONT NECKBAND

With RS facing, using size 9 (5.5mm) needles and MC, pick up and knit 16 sts down left side of front neck, 9 (11: 13) sts from Back, then 16 sts up left side of back neck. 41 (43: 45) sts.

Complete as given for Armhole Borders from ***.

Lay front shoulder over back shoulder so that bound-off edge of Front matches shoulder line. Sew on buttons.

Using photograph as a guide and CC DOUBLE, embroider backstitch heart to Pocket. Sew Pocket to Front as in photograph.

Mittens

Which sizes?
The finished mittens measure 6 (6¼)in/
15 (16)cm around palm of hand.

Which yarns?
BOY'S MITTENS
1 x 50g/1¾oz ball of Jaeger *Matchmaker
Merino DK* in each of **MC** (Mushroom
880) and **CC** (Loden 730)
GIRL'S MITTENS
1 x 50g/1¾oz balls of Jaeger
Matchmaker Merino DK in each of **MC**
(Petal 883) and **CC** (Rock Rose 896)

Which needles?
Pair of size 3 (3.25mm) knitting needles
Pair of size 6 (4mm) knitting needles

What gauge?
22 sts and 30 rows to 4in/10cm
measured over st st using size 6 (4mm)
needles *or size to obtain correct gauge.*

Abbreviations?
See page 125.

These mittens are really great for cold days, but if you don't want your children to lose theirs, it is a good idea to attach a knitted cord to them (use leftover yarn and make it on an old-fashioned knitting spool, see page 123). You then run the cord through their coat sleeves.

These mittens come in the usual two color versions, one for him and one for her, with the ribbed cuffs in a toning shade.

They aren't at all difficult to knit and make a good project for a novice knitter, because they provide practice at some basic shaping.

Right mitten

Using size 3 (3.25mm) needles and CC, cast on
30 (34) sts.

Row 1 (WS) K2, *P2, K2, rep from * to end.

Row 2 P2, *K2, P2, rep from * to end.

These 2 rows form rib.

Work in rib for 12 rows more, ending with RS facing for
next row.

Break off CC and join in MC.

Change to size 6 (4mm) needles.

Starting with a K row, work in st st as foll:

Work 4 rows, ending with RS facing for next row.

SHAPE THUMB GUSSET

Row 1 (RS) K15 (17), M1, K2, M1, K13 (15).

Work 1 row.

Row 3 K15 (17), M1, K4, M1, K13 (15).

Work 1 row.

Row 5 K15 (17), M1, K6, M1, K13 (15).

Work 1 row.

Row 7 K15 (17), M1, K8, M1, K13 (15). 38 (42) sts.

Work 1 row.

Second size only

Row 9 K17, M1, K10, M1, K15. 44 sts.

Work 1 row.

Both sizes

SHAPE THUMB

Next row (RS) K25 (30) and turn.

**Next row Cast on and P 2 sts, P9 (12) and turn.

Work on this set of sts only for thumb.

Cast on 2 sts at beg of next row. 13 (16) sts.

Work 9 (11) rows, ending with RS facing for next row.

Next row (RS) K1 (0), [skp] 6 (8) times. 7 (8) sts.

Work 1 row.

Break off yarn and thread through rem 7 (8) sts. Pull up
tight and fasten off securely. Sew thumb seam.

With RS facing, pick up and knit 3 (4) sts from base of
thumb, K to end. 32 (36) sts.

Work 11 (13) rows, ending with RS facing for next row.

SHAPE TOP

Row 1 (RS) K2, [skp, K9 (11), K2tog, K2] twice. 28 (32) sts.

Work 1 row.

Row 3 K2, [skp, K7 (9), K2tog, K2] twice. 24 (28) sts.

Work 1 row.

Row 5 K2, [skp, K5 (7), K2tog, K2] twice. 20 (24) sts.

Work 1 row. Bind off.

Left mitten

Work as given for Right Mitten to start of thumb gusset
shaping.

SHAPE THUMB GUSSET

Row 1 (RS) K13 (15), M1, K2, M1, K15 (17).

Work 1 row.

Row 3 K13 (15), M1, K4, M1, K15 (17).

Work 1 row.

Row 5 K13 (15), M1, K6, M1, K15 (17).

Work 1 row.

Row 7 K13 (15), M1, K8, M1, K15 (17). 38 (42) sts.

Work 1 row.

Second size only

Row 9 K15, M1, K10, M1, K17. 44 sts.

Work 1 row.

Both sizes

SHAPE THUMB

Next row (RS) K22 (26) and turn.

Complete as given for Right Mitten from **.

Finishing

Press lightly following instructions on yarn label.

Sew side and top seam.

Wrap skirt

This is the perfect little skirt because it wraps around very generously with a tie waist, in a neat A-line shape. It accommodates varying figure shapes and, at the same time, offers lots of room for energetic little girls to run and jump around. Wear it with a T-shirt in spring, and with a warm jacket and thick tights in the winter.

Again, it is very easy to knit, but will require a little more patience than the smaller designs in the book and you will need to make a buttonhole for the waistband (see pages 121 and 122).

The skirt is knitted in Rowan's pure wool *Scottish Tweed* yarn, which may benefit from being washed after knitting because it softens up beautifully after washing.

Which sizes?

To fit ages

3–4	4–5	5–6	years

FINISHED MEASUREMENTS

Around waist

21½	23¼	24¾	in
55	59	63	cm

Length from waist

13¼	15¾	18	in
34	40	46	cm

Which yarns?

2 (2: 3) x 50g/1¾oz balls of Rowan *Scottish Tweed DK* in each of **MC** (Lewis Grey 007) and **A** (Grey Mist 001)

1 x 25g/⅞oz ball of Rowan *Scottish Tweed 4 ply* in **B** (Rose 026)

Which needles?

Pair of size 5 (3.75mm) knitting needles
Pair of size 6 (4mm) knitting needles

What extras?

2 buttons

What gauge?

22 sts and 30 rows to 4in/10cm measured over st st using MC and size 6 (4mm) needles *or size to obtain correct gauge.*

Abbreviations?

See page 125.

Back

Using size 5 (3.75m) needles and A, cast on 91 (101: 111) sts.

Work in garter st (K every row) for 3 rows, ending with RS facing for next row.

Change to size 6 (4mm) needles.

Starting with a K row, work in st st for 4 rows, ending with RS facing for next row.

Next row (RS) K6, skp, K to last 8 sts, K2tog, K6.

Working all side seam decreases as set by last row, dec 1 st at each end of 6th and every foll 6th row until 81 (89: 97) sts rem.

Work 1 row, ending with RS facing for next row.

Break off A and join in B DOUBLE.

Next row (RS) Using B DOUBLE, knit.

Break off B and join in MC.

Starting with a P row, cont in st st, dec 1 st at each end of 4th and every foll 6th row until 61 (65: 69) sts rem, ending with **WS** facing for next row.**

Next row (WS) Cast on and K 4 sts (for button band), P to end. 65 (69: 73) sts.

Next row Knit.

Next row K4, P to end.

Rep last 2 rows twice more, ending with RS facing for next row.

Change to size 5 (3.75mm) needles.

Next row (RS) P1, *K1, P1, rep from * to last 4 sts, K4.

Next row K5, *P1, K1, rep from * to end.

Rep last 2 rows 3 times more.

Bind off in patt.

Front

Work as given for Back to **.

Next row (WS) P to last 4 sts, K4.

Next row Knit.

Rep last 2 rows once more, then first of these 2 rows

again, ending with RS facing for next row.

Next row (RS) K2, yo (to make a buttonhole), K2tog, K to end.

Next row P to last 4 sts, K4.

Change to size 5 (3.75mm) needles.

Next row (RS) K4, P1, *K1, P1, rep from * to end.

Next row *K1, P1, rep from * to last 5 sts, K5.

These 2 rows set the sts—left side seam 4 sts in garter st with all other sts in rib.

Cont as set for 2 rows more.

Next row (RS) K2, yo (to make second buttonhole), K2tog, P1, *K1, P1, rep from * to end.

Work 3 rows more, ending with RS facing for next row.

Bind off in patt.

Finishing

Press lightly on **WS** following instructions on yarn label. Sew side seams, leaving left side seam open for last 15 rows. Sew cast-on edge of button band in place on inside. Sew on buttons.

BELT

Using size 5 (3.75mm) needles and A, cast on 7 sts.

Row 1 (RS) K2, P1, K1, P1, K2.

Row 2 K1, [P1, K1] 3 times.

Rep these 2 rows until Belt measures 35½ (37½: 39¼)in/ 90 (95: 100)cm, ending with RS facing for next row.

Bind off in rib.

Mark center of Belt. Lay Belt around waist edge of skirt so that center falls along right side seam. Matching one row-end edge of Belt to bound-off edge of skirt, sew Belt in place by stitching through all layers along right side seam.

Fisherman's scarves

How big?
The finished scarf measures 5in/13cm wide and 38½in/98cm long, excluding fringe.

Which yarns?
GIRL'S SCARF
2 x 50g/1¾oz balls of Rowan *Big Wool* in **A** (Whoosh 014)
2 x 50g/1¾oz balls of Jaeger *Baby Merino 4 ply* in **B** (Red Cheek 094)
BOY'S SCARF
2 x 50g/1¾oz balls of Rowan *Big Wool* in **A** (Zing 037)
2 x 50g/1¾oz balls of Jaeger *Matchmaker Merino 4 ply* in **B** (Flannel 782)

Which needles?
Pair of size 10 (6mm) knitting needles

What gauge?
16 sts and 31 rows to 4in/10cm measured over patt using size 10 (6mm) needles *or size to obtain correct gauge.*

Abbreviations?
K1 below = K into next st one row below at same time slipping off st above.
See also page 125.

This scarf comes in two colors, one for him and one for her, and is knitted in Rowan's *Big Wool* and Jaeger *Merino 4 ply*. The interesting textural effect and intermingling of yarns is created by knitting into every other stitch in the row below. This stitch pattern makes the scarves really warm, too. The fringed ends are made with the thicker yarn.

Jayden wears the boy's green version with his matching balaclava and animal picture sweater. Abi grabbed both to play with, and her dolly seemed to enjoy the experience!

Scarf

Using size 10 (6mm) needles and A, cast on 20 sts.

Row 1 (WS) Knit.

Now work in patt as foll:

Row 1 Using A, sl 1, *K1 below, K1, rep from * to last st, K1.

Join in B.

Rows 2 and 3 Using B, sl 1, *K1 below, K1, rep from * to last st, K1.

Row 4 As row 1.

These 4 rows form patt.

Cont in patt until Scarf measures 38½in/98cm, ending after patt row 4.

Bind off in patt.

Finishing

Do NOT press.

Cut 40 lengths of A, each 13¾in/35cm long. Knot groups of 4 of these lengths through ends of Scarf to form fringe, positioning 5 knots evenly across each end.

HOME COMFORTS

Cabled sweater and scarf

This cabled sweater is a great design for lounging around at home, as well as for wearing outside, and the denim yarn has a really nice feel, too. The crew neck sits quite low, with a nice rolled edge, which works well with a T-shirt or a shirt. It looks equally good on both boys and girls. The toning cabled scarf is definitely for outdoor use but Abi insisted on wearing it indoors as well!

Although cables are perhaps a little more complicated than some of the other stitches in this book, they aren't difficult and we give some tips on how to work them on page 123.

Which sizes?

SWEATER

To fit ages

3–4	4–5	5–6	years

FINISHED MEASUREMENTS

Around chest

25½	27½	29½	in
65	70	75	cm

Length from shoulder

13¼	14 1/2	15¾	in
34	37	40	cm

Sleeve seam

9¾	11	12¼	in
25	28	31	cm

SCARF

The finished scarf measures 4¾in/12cm wide
and 39¼in/100cm long.

Which yarns?

SWEATER

6 (7: 8) x 50g/1¾oz balls of Rowan *Denim*
in **A** (Memphis 229) and 1 (1: 1) ball in
B (Tennessee 231)

SCARF

3 x 50g/1¾oz balls of Rowan *Denim*
in **A** (Tennessee 231) and 1 ball in
B (Memphis 229)

Which needles?

Pair of size 5 (3.75mm) knitting needles
Pair of size 6 (4mm) knitting needles
Cable needle

What gauge?

After washing: 22 sts and 28 rows to
4in/10cm measured over st st using size 6
(4mm) needles *or size to obtain correct
gauge.*

Note: Rowan *Denim* will shrink in length
when washed for the first time. Allowances
have been made in the pattern for
shrinkage.

Abbreviations?

C10B = slip next 5 sts onto cable needle and
leave at back of work, K5, then K5 from
cable needle.
See also page 125.

SWEATER

Back

Using size 5 (3.75mm) needles and B, cast on
82 (86: 94) sts.
Row 1 (RS) K2, *P2, K2, rep from * to end.
Row 2 P2, *K2, P2, rep from * to end.
These 2 rows form rib.
Break off B and join in A.
Work in rib for 16 rows more, inc 0 (1: 0) st at
each end of last row and ending with RS facing
for next row. 82 (88: 94) sts.
Change to size 6 (4mm) needles.
Cont in patt as foll:
Row 1 (RS) P16 (19: 22), K10, (P10, K10) twice,
P to end.
Row 2 K16 (19: 22), P10, (K10, P10) twice, K
to end.
Rows 3 to 12 As rows 1 and 2, 5 times.
Row 13 P16 (19: 22), C10B, (P10, C10B) twice,
P to end.
Row 14 As row 2.
Rows 15 and 16 As rows 1 and 2.
These 16 rows form patt.
Work even in patt until Back measures
9¾ (10½: 11¾)in/25 (27: 30)cm, ending with
RS facing for next row.
SHAPE ARMHOLES
Keeping patt correct, bind off 6 (7: 8) sts at beg
of next 2 rows. 70 (74: 78) sts.
Work even until armhole measures 5 (5½:
6)in/13 (14: 15)cm, ending with RS facing for
next row.
SHAPE BACK NECK
Next row (RS) Patt 22 (23: 24) sts and turn,
leaving rem sts on a holder.

Work each side of neck separately.

Dec 1 st at neck edge of next 4 rows. 18 (19: 20) sts.

Work 3 rows, ending with RS facing for next row.

SHAPE SHOULDER

Bind off.

With RS facing, rejoin yarn to rem sts, P8 (9: 10), K1, [K2tog] 4 times, K1, P8 (9: 10) and slip these 22 (24: 26) sts onto a holder, patt to end. 22 (23: 24) sts.

Complete to match first side, reversing shapings.

Front

Work as given for Back until armhole measures 3 (3½: 4)in/8 (9: 10)cm, ending with RS facing for next row.

SHAPE FRONT NECK

Next row (RS) Patt 27 (28: 29) sts and turn, leaving rem sts on a holder.

Work each side of neck separately.

Dec 1 st at neck edge of next 9 rows. 18 (19: 20) sts.

Work even until Front matches Back to shoulder bind-off, ending with RS facing for next row.

SHAPE SHOULDER

Bind off.

With RS facing, rejoin yarn to rem sts, P2 (3: 4), K1, [K2tog] 4 times, K1, P2 (3: 4) and slip these 12 (14: 16) sts onto a holder, patt to end. 27 (28: 29) sts.

Complete to match first side, reversing shapings.

Sleeves

Using size 5 (3.75mm) needles and B, cast on 38 (42: 46) sts.

Work in rib as given for Back for 2 rows, ending with RS facing for next row.

Break off B and join in A.

Work in rib for 14 rows more, ending with RS facing for next row.

Change to size 6 (4mm) needles.

Starting with a P row, work in rev st st, shaping sides by inc 1 st at each end of 3rd (5th: 7th) and every foll 6th row until there are 56 (62: 66) sts.

Work even until Sleeve measures 11½ (12½: 14)in/29 (32: 36)cm, ending with RS facing for next row.

SHAPE TOP OF SLEEVE

Mark both ends of last row to denote top of sleeve seam.

Work 6 (8: 10) rows more, ending with RS facing for next row. Bind off.

Finishing

Do NOT press.

Sew right shoulder seam.

NECKBAND

With RS facing, using size 5 (3.75mm) needles and B, pick up and knit 17 sts down left side of front neck, K across 12 (14: 16) sts on Front holder, pick up and knit 17 sts up right side of front neck, and 7 sts down right side of back neck, K across 22 (24: 26) sts on Back holder, then pick up and knit 7 sts up left side of back neck. 82 (86: 90) sts.

Starting with P row, work in st st for 10 rows, ending with **WS** facing for next row.

Bind off purlwise (on **WS**).

Sew left shoulder and Neckband seam, reversing Neckband seam for st st roll. Matching sleeve markers to top of side seams and center of sleeve bound-off edge to shoulder seams, sew Sleeves into armholes. Sew side and sleeve seams.

Hot machine wash and tumble dry garment (to shrink it to correct size), then press lightly on **WS** following instructions on yarn label and avoiding ribbing.

SCARF

Using size 5 (3.75mm) needles and B, cast on 38 sts.
Starting with a K row, work in st st for 8 rows, ending with RS facing for next row.
Break off B and join in A.
Change to size 6 (4mm) needles.
Cont in patt as foll:
Row 1 (RS) K2, P3, K10, P8, K10, P3, K2.
Row 2 K5, P10, K8, P10, K5.
Rows 3 to 12 As rows 1 and 2, 5 times.
Row 13 K2, P3, C10B, P8, C10B, P3, K2.
Row 14 As row 2.
Rows 15 and 16 As rows 1 and 2.
These 16 rows form patt.
Work even in patt until Scarf measures 43¼in/110cm,
ending after patt row 8 and with RS facing for next row.
Break off A and join in B.
Change to size 5 (3.75mm) needles.
Starting with a K row, work in st st for 8 rows, ending with RS facing for next row.
Bind off.

Finishing

Do NOT press.
Hot machine wash and tumble dry (to shrink it to correct size), then press lightly on **WS** following instructions on yarn label.

Textured pillow cover

How big?
The finished cushion cover fits a 13¾in/35cm square pillow form.

Which yarns?
5 x 50g/1¾oz balls of Rowan *RYC Cashsoft DK* in **A** (Sweet 501), and 1 ball in **B** (Cream 500)

Which needles?
Pair of size 9 (5.5mm) knitting needles

What gauge?
16 sts and 22 rows to 4in/10cm measured over st st using yarn DOUBLE and size 9 (5.5mm) needles *or size to obtain correct gauge.*

Abbreviations?
See page 125.

This is a super-soft pillow for the nursery, knitted in Rowan's *RYC cashsoft DK*. It has a pretty textured pattern made from self stripes of garter stitch and stockinette and reversed stockinette stitch. The pillow has a simple fold-over back, with a ribbed back opening, edged in cream. It makes a great first knitting project, since it is really very simple to make and has no shaping whatsoever.

As it is not at all difficult to knit, why not make two or three in toning colorways? The mouse slippers shown with it are featured on pages 82 and 83.

Pillow cover

Using size 9 (5.5mm) needles and B DOUBLE, cast on 56 sts.

Row 1 (WS) Knit.

Break off B and join in A DOUBLE.

Starting with a K row, work in st st for 10 rows, ending with RS facing for next row.

Starting with a P row, work in rev st st for 32 rows, ending with RS facing for next row.

Place blue markers at both ends of last row.

Work in rev st st for 32 rows more, ending with RS facing for next row.

Starting with a K row, work in st st for 10 rows, ending with RS facing for next row.

Starting with a P row, work in rev st st for 14 rows, ending with RS facing for next row.

Starting with a K row, work in st st for 10 rows, ending with RS facing for next row.

Starting with a P row, work in rev st st for 32 rows, ending with RS facing for next row.

Place red markers at both ends of last row.

Work 50 rows more, ending with RS facing for next row.

Bind off.

Finishing

Press lightly following instructions on yarn label. With RS together, fold cast-on edge up onto center section along row marked by blue markers. Fold bound-off edge over these by folding along row marked by red markers. Sew side seams. Turn pillow cover RS out.

Roll-up mat

Abi goes to quite a few sleepovers, and this little stripy mat is the ideal thing to take to a friend's house overnight. It is knitted in Rowan *Handknit Cotton*, filled with a thinnish layer of foam rubber (or thick polyester batting) and backed with a striped cotton fabric. It rolls up quickly and easily, and is really light to carry. A knitted tie secures the roll.

When not used as a sleeping mat, it makes a good playmat or rug for a wooden nursery floor. Or, if your child is into yoga, it makes a great exercise mat as well.

How big?

The finished mat measures 4¾in/12cm wide and 90cm/35½in long.

Which yarns?

7 x 50g/1¾oz balls of Rowan *Handknit Cotton* in **A** (Celery 309), 3 balls in each of **D** (Mojito 322) and **G** (Chime 205), 2 balls in **F** (Flame 254), and 1 ball in each of **B** (Linen 205), **C** (Slippery 316), and **E** (Ecru 251)

Which needles?

Pair of size 6 (4mm) knitting needles

What extras?

Piece of 2.5cm/1in thick foam rubber (or thick polyester batting) to fit mat size
Piece of backing fabric to fit mat size
Matching sewing thread

What gauge?

20 sts and 28 rows to 4in/10cm measured over rev st st using size 6 (4mm) needles *or size to obtain correct gauge.*

Abbreviations?

See page 125.

Mat

Using size 6 (4mm) needles and A, cast on 140 sts.
Joining in and breaking off colors as required and starting with a P row, work in rev st st in stripes as foll:
Rows 1 to 49 Using A.
Rows 50 to 56 Using B.
Rows 57 to 91 Using A.
Rows 92 to 98 Using C.
Rows 99 to 147 Using D.
Rows 148 to 154 Using E.
Rows 155 to 157 Using F.
Rows 158 to 185 Using G.
Rows 186 to 190 Using D.

Rows 191 to 218 Using A.
Rows 219 to 225 Using E.
Rows 226 to 295 Using A.
Rows 296 to 305 Using F.
Rows 306 to 354 Using G.
Rows 355 to 359 Using A.
Rows 360 to 391 Using D.
Bind off knitwise (on **WS**).

Tie

Using size 6 (4mm) needles and F, cast on 7 sts. Work in garter st (K every row) until Tie measures 55in/140cm. Bind off.

Finishing

Press lightly following instructions on yarn label. Trim foam rubber (or batting) to same size as knitted piece. Trim backing fabric to same size as knitted piece, plus a seam allowance all around edges. Fold seam allowance to **WS** around edges of backing fabric. Lay knitted Mat flat, **WS** uppermost. Lay foam rubber (or batting) on knitted piece, then cover with backing fabric, RS uppermost. Sew backing fabric and knitted piece together around entire outer edge, enclosing foam rubber (or batting).

Animal slippers

My daughter refuses to be parted from her slippers, and I can't say I blame her. They are great fun. Your child can choose between the fierce stripy Tiger Toes slippers or the sweeter Mouse Ears version. They both have a similar comfy square-toed shape and a cute face on the front, and both have ears with a contrasting colored inside.

Made simply in garter stitch, they can be knitted in no time at all, so even if you have never knitted much before, you will be able to make these easily. Only some simple embroidery skills and a blunt-ended needle are needed to create the faces.

Which sizes?
To fit ages

| 1–2 | 2–3 | 3–4 | years |

Which yarns?
TIGER TOES SLIPPERS

1 x 50g/1¾oz ball of Rowan *Kid Classic* in each of **A** (Sandstone 849), **B** (Feather 828), and **C** (Bear 817)

MOUSE EARS SLIPPERS

1 x 50g/1¾oz ball of Rowan *Kid Classic* in each of **A** (Sherbet Dip 850) and **B** (Crystal 840)

Which needles?
Pair of size 9 (5.5mm) knitting needles

What extras?
4 buttons (for eyes)

MOUSE EARS SLIPPERS ONLY

Scrap of white felt (for eye backing)

WHAT GAUGE?
15 sts and 30 rows to 4in/10cm measured over garter st using size 9 (5.5mm) needles *or size to obtain correct gauge.*

Abbreviations?
See page 125.

TIGER TOES SLIPPERS

Main section

Using size 9 (5.5mm) needles and A, cast on 18 (21: 24) sts.

Work in garter st (K every row) for 4¾ (5½: 6¼)in/12 (14: 16)cm, ending with RS facing for next row.*

Using A, B, and C at random and changing color after RS rows (so that color change forms a broken line on RS), cont in striped garter st until work measures 9½ (11: 12½)in/24 (28: 32)cm, ending with RS facing for next row.

Bind off.

Heel section

Using size 9 (5.5mm) needles and A, cast on 18 (21: 24) sts.

Using A, B, and C at random and changing color after RS rows (so that color change forms a broken line on RS), work in striped garter st for 4¾ (5½: 6¼)in/12 (14: 16)cm, ending with RS facing for next row.

Bind off.

Ears (make 2)

Using size 9 (5.5mm) needles and A, cast on 4 sts.

**Work in garter st, inc 1 st at each end of 3rd and foll alt row. 8 sts.

Work 3 rows, ending with RS facing for next row.

Dec 1 st at each end of next and foll alt row. 4 sts.

Work 1 row, ending with RS facing for next row.**

Break off A and join in B.

Rep from ** to ** once more.

Bind off.

Finishing

Do NOT press.

Fold Main Section in half so that it forms a square—one

side is striped, other side is plain. Lay folded square flat with plain side uppermost and fold 3 corners in to the center of the square, to form an open envelope shape. Sew seams where the edges meet—this section forms toe of slipper. (Heel of slipper is the remaining free point of Main Section.)

***Fold Heel Section in half to form a triangle. Leaving the folded edge free (to form heel opening edge of slipper), sew other 2 edges of Heel Section to remaining 2 edges of Main Section—ends of folded edge of Heel Section meet joined corners of Main Section on top of foot.

Fold Ears in half and sew row-end edges together, leaving cast-on and bound-off edges open. Make a small pleat in cast-on/bound-off edges, then sew Ears to slipper as in photograph.***

Using photograph as a guide, sew on buttons to form eyes. Using C, embroider satin st nose and backstitch W-shape to form mouth. Using B, embroider satin st tongue.

MOUSE EARS SLIPPERS

Main section
Work as given for Main Section of Tiger Toes Slippers to *.
Break off A and join in B.
Cont in garter st (K every row) until work measures

9½ (11: 12½)in24 (28: 32)cm/, ending with RS facing for next row. Bind off.

Heel section

Work as given for Heel Section of Tiger Toes Slippers but using B throughout.

Ears (make 2)

Work as given for Ears of Tiger Toes Slippers.

Finishing

Do NOT press.

Fold Main Section in half so that it forms a square—one side is in A, other side is in B. Lay folded square flat with side in A uppermost and fold 3 corners in to the center of the square, to form an open envelope shape. Sew seams where the edges meet—this section forms toe of slipper. (Heel of slipper is the remaining free point of Main Section.)

Work as for Tiger Toes Slippers from *** to ***.

From felt, cut out circles slightly larger than buttons. Lay a button on a felt circle (to form completed eye) and then using photograph as a guide, sew eyes to slippers. Using A, embroider satin st nose. For whiskers, cut 2¾in/7cm lengths of B and knot through slippers at each side of nose as in photograph.

Herb pillows

This lavender-filled neck pillow is perfect for those times—for example, when flying at night on holiday or on a long car journey—when you want your child to settle down and relax. Or, indeed, when you need to do just that yourself, after looking after him or her!

It comes in two versions, a plain one and a striped one, both in the wonderfully soft and soothing Rowan *Cashcotton*.

Both of them are extremely easy to knit, so are perfect for a first time project, although you will have to make a little fabric liner to go inside the pillow for the lavender and stuffing.

How big?
The finished pillow measures 6in/15cm wide and 19½in/50cm long.

Which yarns?
PLAIN PILLOW
1 x 50g/1¾oz ball of Rowan *RYC Cashcotton 4 ply* in **A** (Cyclamen 911) and 2 balls in **B** (Chintz 906)
STRIPED PILLOW
1 x 50g/1¾oz ball of Rowan *RYC Cashcotton 4 ply* in each of **A** (Geranium 604), **B** (Cork 904), and **C** (Sea Foam 903)

Which needles?
Pair of size 3 (3.25mm) knitting needles

What extras?
Piece of fabric to make a liner, lavender, and washable stuffing

What gauge?
23 sts and 53 rows to 4in/10cm measured over patt using size 3 (3.25mm) needles *or size to obtain correct gauge.*

Abbreviations?
K1 below = K into next st one row below at same time slipping off st above. See also page 125.

PLAIN PILLOW

Using size 3 (3.25mm) needles and A, cast on
35 sts. Break off A and join in B.
Row 2 (WS) Using B, knit.
Now work in patt as foll:
Row 1 Using B, sl 2, *K1, K1 below, rep from *
to end.
Row 2 using B, sl 1, *K1, K1 below, rep from *
to last 2 stits, K2.
Continue in patt until Pillow measures
41in/104cm, ending with RS facing for next row.
Bind off in patt.
Finish as for Striped Pillow.

STRIPED PILLOW

Using size 3 (3.25mm) needles and A, cast on
35 sts.
Break off A and join in B.
Row 1 (WS) Using B, knit.
Now work in patt as foll:
Row 1 Using B, sl 1, *K1 below, K1, rep from *
to end.
Row 2 Using B, sl 1, *K1, K1 below, rep from *
to last 2 sts, K2.
Rows 3 to 24 As rows 1 and 2, 11 times.
Join in C.
Rows 25 to 48 As rows 1 and 2, 12 times but
using C.
These 48 rows form patt.
Cont in patt until Pillow measures 41in/104cm,
ending with RS facing for next row.
Bind off in patt.

Finishing

Do NOT press.

With RS together, fold cast-on edge up onto center section, making fold approximately 9¾in/25cm from cast-on edge. Fold bound-off edge over these so that distance between folds is 19½in/50cm. Sew side seams. Turn pillow RS out.

From lining fabric, cut out 2 pieces same size as completed neck pillow, plus a seam allowance all around edges. Sew together pieces along all 4 sides, leaving a small opening. Mix together lavender and stuffing, then insert inside lining. Sew opening closed. Slip pillow inside knitted section.

His and hers socks

These socks are knitted in Rowan *Wool Cotton*, which washes well but feels cozy and soft to the touch. The girl's version has a pretty picot edging in a contrasting color, used for the toe as well, while the boy's version is also in *Wool Cotton*, but striped in blues and grays.

These socks are knitted on four needles, which isn't particularly difficult once you get the hang of it (see page 122), although you need to be careful not to let the stitches slide off the needles.

Turning a heel on socks baffles some people, so we have explained this a little more clearly on page 93.

Which sizes?

GIRL'S SOCKS

The finished socks measure 6 (6½)in/15 (17)cm from heel to toe, and 5¾ (6½)in/14.5 (16.5)cm around foot.

BOY'S STRIPED SOCKS

The finished socks measure 6 (6½)in/15 (16.5)cm from heel to toe, and 5¾ (6½)in/14.5 (16.5)cm around foot.

Which yarns?

GIRL'S SOCKS

2 x 50g/1¾oz balls of Rowan *Wool Cotton* in **MC** (Hiss 952) and 1 ball in **CC** (Bilberry Fool 959)

BOY'S STRIPED SOCKS

1 x 50g/1¾oz balls of Rowan *Wool Cotton* in each of **MC** (Moonstone 961) and **CC** (Aloof 958)

Which needles?

Set of 4 double-pointed size 6 (4mm) knitting needles

What gauge?

22 sts and 30 rows to 4in/10cm measured over st st using size 6 (4mm) needles *or size to obtain correct gauge*.

Abbreviations?

See page 125.

GIRL'S SOCKS (both alike)

Using size 6 (4mm) needles and CC, work picot cast-on as foll: *cast on 5 sts, bind off 2 sts, slip st now on right needle back onto left needle, rep from * until there are 39 (42) sts on left needle.

Distribute these sts evenly over 3 needles.

Working in rounds, cont as foll:

Round 1 (RS) Purl.

Break off CC and join in MC.

Now work in rounds of st st as foll:

Round 1 Knit.

This round forms st st.

Work in st st for 21 (23) rounds more.

Next round K6, K2tog, K to last 8 sts, skp, K6. 37 (40) sts.

Work 7 (9) rounds.

Next round K5, K2tog, K to last 7 sts, skp, K5. 35 (38) sts.

Work 7 (9) rounds.

Next round K4, K2tog, K to last 6 sts, skp, K4. 33 (36) sts.

Work 7 (9) rounds.

First size only

Next round K15, K2tog, K15. 32 sts.

Both sizes

Break off yarn.

SHAPE HEEL

Re-arrange sts on needles as foll: slip first and last 9 (10) sts of last round onto one needle—these will be used for heel, and distribute rem 14 (16) sts evenly over 2 other needles.

With **WS** facing, rejoin MC to heel 18 (20) sts.

Working in rows of st st, starting with a P row, work heel as foll:

Work 9 rows, ending with RS facing for next row.

Row 10 (RS) K13 (15), skp and turn.

Row 11 Sl 1, P8 (10), P2tog and turn.

Row 12 Sl 1, K8 (10), skp and turn.

Rep rows 11 and 12 twice more, then row 11 again.
10 (12) sts.

Break off yarn.

SHAPE FOOT

Re-arrange sts on 3 needles as foll: slip first 5 (6) sts of heel onto 3rd needle, rem 5 (6) sts onto first needle, and 14 (16) sts of leg onto 2nd needle.

With RS facing, rejoin MC to sts on first needle.

Working in rounds of st st, work foot as foll:

Round 1 (RS) K 5 (6) sts from first needle, pick up and knit 8 sts down first side of heel, K 14 (16) sts from 2nd needle, using next needle pick up and K 8 sts up second side of heel, then K 5 (6) sts from 3rd needle. 40 (44) sts.

Work 1 round.

Round 3 K11 (12), K2tog, K14 (16), K2tog tbl, K11 (12). 38 (42) sts.

Work 1 round.

Round 5 K10 (11), K2tog, K14 (16), K2tog tbl, K10 (11). 36 (40) sts.

Work 1 round.

Round 7 K9 (10), K2tog, K14 (16), K2tog tbl, K9 (10). 34 (38) sts.

Work 1 round.

Round 9 K8 (9), K2tog, K14 (16), K2tog tbl, K8 (9). 32 (36) sts.

Work 20 (26) rounds.

SHAPE TOE

Round 1 K5 (6), K2tog, K2, skp, K10 (12), K2tog, K2, skp, K5 (6). 28 (32) sts.

Work 1 round.

Break off MC and cont using CC only.

Round 3 K4 (5), K2tog, K2, skp, K8 (10), K2tog, K2, skp, K4 (5). 24 (28) sts.

Work 1 round.

Round 5 K3 (4), K2tog, K2, skp, K6 (8), K2tog, K2, skp, K3 (4). 20 (24) sts.

Work 1 round.

Round 7 K2 (3), K2tog, K2, skp, K4 (6), K2tog, K2, skp, K2 (3). 16 (20) sts.

Work 1 round.

Break off CC.

Slip first and last 4 (5) sts onto one needle, and rem 10 (12) sts onto another needle.

Turn Sock inside out and, using a 3rd needle and CC, bind off sts on both needles together to form toe seam.

Finishing

Press lightly following instructions on yarn label.

BOY'S STRIPED SOCKS (both alike)

Using size 6 (4mm) needles and CC, cast on 40 (44) sts and distribute these sts evenly over 3 needles.

Working in rounds, cont as foll:

Round 1 (RS) *K1, P1, rep from * to end.

This round forms rib.

Work in rib for 5 (7) rounds more, ending with RS facing for next round.

Join in MC.

Now work in rounds of striped st st as foll:

Rounds 1 to 5 Using MC, knit.

Round 6 Using CC, knit.

These 6 rounds form striped st st.

Work in striped st st for 16 (18) rounds more, ending after 4 (1) rounds using MC (CC).

Keeping stripes correct, cont as foll:

Next round K6, K2tog, K to last 8 sts, skp, K6. 38 (42) sts.

Work 7 (9) rounds.

Next round K5, K2tog, K to last 7 sts, skp, K5. 36 (40) sts.

Work 7 (9) rounds.

Next round K4, K2tog, K to last 6 sts, skp, K4. 34 (38) sts.

Work 7 (9) rounds.

Next round K3, K2tog, K to last 5 sts, skp, K3. 32 (36) sts.

Work 1 round, ending after 1 (2) rounds using CC (MC).
Break off yarns.

SHAPE HEEL

Re-arrange sts on needles as foll: slip first and last 9 (10) sts of last round onto one needle—these will be used for heel, and distribute rem 14 (16) sts evenly over 2 other needles.

With RS facing, rejoin CC to heel 18 (20) sts.

Working in rows of st st using CC only, starting with a K row, work heel as foll:

Work 10 rows, ending with RS facing for next row.

Row 11 (RS) K13 (15), skp and turn.

Row 12 sl 1, P8 (10), P2tog and turn.

Row 13 sl 1, K8 (10), skp and turn.

Rep rows 12 and 13 twice more, then row 12 again. 10 (12) sts.

Break off CC.

SHAPE FOOT

Re-arrange sts on 3 needles as foll: slip first 5 (6) sts of heel onto 3rd needle, rem 5 (6) sts onto first needle, and 14 (16) sts of foot of leg onto 2nd needle.

With RS facing, rejoin MC to sts on first needle.

Working in rounds of striped st st, starting with 5 (3) rows using MC, work foot as foll:

Round 1 (RS) K 5 (6) sts from first needle, pick up and knit 8 sts down first side of heel, K 14 (16) sts from 2nd needle, using next needle pick up and K 8 sts up second side of heel, then K 5 (6) sts from 3rd needle. 40 (44) sts.

Round 2 K11 (12), K2tog, K14 (16), K2tog tbl, K11 (12). 38 (42) sts.

Work 1 round.

Round 4 K10 (11), K2tog, K14 (16), K2tog tbl, K10 (11). 36 (40) sts.

Work 1 round.

Round 6 K9 (10), K2tog, K14 (16), K2tog tbl, K9 (10). 34 (38) sts.

Work 1 round.

Round 8 K8 (9), K2tog, K14 (16), K2tog tbl, K8 (9). 32 (36) sts.

Work 20 (24) rounds, ending after 5 rounds using MC.
Break off MC and cont using CC only.

SHAPE TOE

Round 1 K5 (6), K2tog, K2, skp, K10 (12), K2tog, K2, skp, K5 (6). 28 (32) sts.

Work 1 round.

Round 3 K4 (5), K2tog, K2, skp, K8 (10), K2tog, K2, skp, K4 (5). 24 (28) sts.

Work 1 round.

Round 5 K3 (4), K2tog, K2, skp, K6 (8), K2tog, K2, skp, K3 (4). 20 (24) sts.

Work 1 round.

Round 7 K2 (3), K2tog, K2, skp, K4 (6), K2tog, K2, skp, K2 (3). 16 (20) sts.

Work 1 round.

Break off CC.

Slip first and last 4 (5) sts onto one needle, and rem 10 (12) sts onto another needle.

Turn Sock inside out and, using a 3rd needle and CC, bind off sts on both needles together to form toe seam.

Finishing

Press lightly following instructions on yarn label.

Tips for knitting socks

Knitting on four needles is discussed on page 122, but when it comes to socks, in addition to mastering knitting with four double-pointed needles instead of two, you also have to be able to "turn" the heel part of the sock. This isn't difficult if you follow the pattern instructions given here carefully, but you may become confused if you do not understand how the heel part of the sock is "turned."

You start at the calf of the sock and knit in rounds downward toward the toe. But when you get to the heel area, you have to divide the knitting, and first work the stitches that will form the heel.

The rest of the knitting is "held" while you work the heel in rows. After the straight section of the heel (the heel flap) is complete, the heel is "turned" with decreases and turned rows.

Next, you pick up stitches along each side of the heel and start working in rounds again with all the stitches, shaping the sock at first to fit the right angle of the ankle.

Lastly, you work the sock without shaping until you reach the toe, where you decrease the stitches to make a neatly rounded toe.

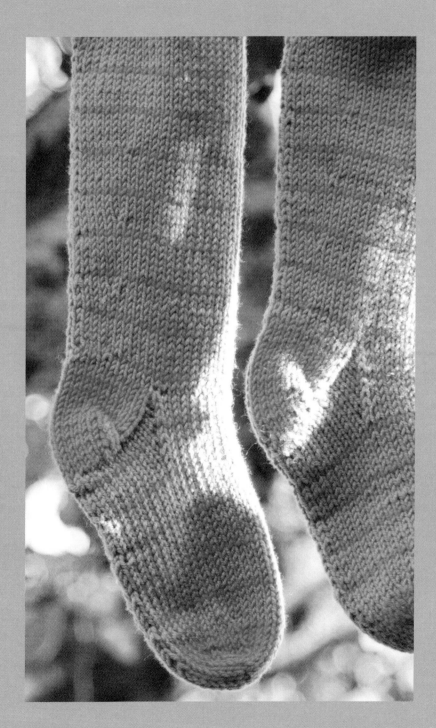

Pen and toy pots

How big?
The finished pen pot is approximately 4¾in/12cm tall, and the finished toy pot is approximately 9¾in/25cm tall.

Which yarns?
PEN POT
1 x 100g/3½oz ball of Rowan *Scottish Tweed Chunky* in each of **A** (Rose 026) and **B** (Porridge 024)
TOY POT
1 x 100g/3½oz ball of Rowan *Scottish Tweed Chunky* in each of **A** (Mallard 020), **B** (Sea Green 006), and **C** (Porridge 024)

Which needles?
Pair of size 10½ (7mm) knitting needles

What gauge?
13 sts and 18 rows to 4in/10cm measured over st st using size 10½ (7mm) needles *or size to obtain correct gauge.*

Abbreviations?
See page 125.

These little pots are made to the same basic design, but the smaller one has fine stripes and the larger one has in three different blocks of color. Both are knitted in Rowan's pure wool *Scottish Tweed Chunky* yarn, which knits up very quick and also felts very well, too. If you machine wash them at 100°F after sewing the seam, they will shrink, making them firm enough to stay upright. You can also insert a cardboard roll inside to give them more body.

Fill them with nursery nicknacks or use them as decoration on their own on a mantelpiece or shelf.

PEN POT

Using **size 10½ (7mm)** needles and A, cast on 29 sts.
Row 1 (WS) Knit.
Starting with a K row, work in striped st st as foll:
Using A, work 2 rows.
Join in B.
Using B, work 2 rows.
These 4 rows form striped st st.
Work in striped st st for 18 rows more, ending after 2 rows using A and with RS facing for next row.
Break off B and cont using A only.
Next row (RS) Purl (to form base fold line).
SHAPE BASE
Row 1 (WS) Purl.
Row 2 [K2, K2tog] 7 times, K1. 22 sts.
Row 3 Purl.
Row 4 [K1, K2tog] 7 times, K1. 15 sts.
Row 5 P1, [P2tog] 7 times. 8 sts.
Row 6 [K2tog] 4 times.
Break yarn and thread through rem 4 sts. Pull up tight and fasten off securely.

TOY POT

Using **size 10½ (7mm)** needles and C, cast on 54 sts.
Row 1 (WS) Knit.
Starting with a K row, work in st st as foll:
Work 6 rows, ending with RS facing for next row.
Break off C and join in B.
Work 2 rows.
Row 9 (RS) K4, *M1, K5, rep from * to end. 64 sts.
Work 9 rows, ending with RS facing for next row.
Break off B and join in A.
Row 19 K4, *M1, K6, rep from * to end. 74 sts.

Work 9 rows.
Row 29 K4, *M1, K7, rep from * to end. 84 sts.
Work 5 rows.
Row 35 K4, *K2tog, K6, rep from * to end. 74 sts.
Work 5 rows.
Row 41 K4, *K2tog, K5, rep from * to end. 64 sts.
Work 3 rows, ending with RS facing for next row.
Next row (RS) Purl (to form base fold line).
Break off A and join in B.
SHAPE BASE
Row 1 (WS) Purl.
Row 2 [K7, K2tog] 7 times, K1. 57 sts.
Row 3 Purl.
Row 4 [K6, K2tog] 7 times, K1. 50 sts.
Row 5 Purl.
Row 6 [K5, K2tog] 7 times, K1. 43 sts.
Row 7 Purl.
Row 8 [K4, K2tog] 7 times, K1. 36 sts.
Row 9 Purl.
Row 10 [K3, K2tog] 7 times, K1. 29 sts.
Row 11 Purl.
Row 12 [K2, K2tog] 7 times, K1. 22 sts.
Row 13 Purl.
Row 14 [K1, K2tog] 7 times, K1. 15 sts.
Row 15 P1, [P2tog] 7 times. 8 sts.
Row 16 [K2tog] 4 times.
Break yarn and thread through rem 4 sts. Pull up tight and fasten off securely.

Finishing
Do NOT press.
Sew back and base seam.
Machine wash at 100°F on a cotton wash cycle (to shrink pot to required size). Once dry, press lightly following instructions on yarn label.

Making circular felted pots

These little pots are very easy to make, and are knitted in stockinette stitch on two needles, in one piece. When completed you have to sew the side and base seams to make the pot shape. The pot in each case is worked by starting at the top of the pot and working downward. When the pot is the right height, you knit a purl row to make a fold line for the base, and then start decreasing on every knit row, as instructed in the pattern, to form the shape.

Once you have knitted and made up the pots you can felt them in the washing machine. All machines vary but generally a 100°F wash will felt the pots down by enough to make a firm texture. If you want a more heavily felted pot, you may have to put them through a second time, in which case you will find it shrinks more.

Striped robe

Knitted in wonderfully soft Rowan *Baby Alpaca DK*, this is a luxury item for a boy or a girl, and will make them feel cozy and secure. Just the thing to put on in the evening after bathtime, while they snuggle up for a bedtime story.

It is the ideal garment for traveling, too, because they can slip it on over a T-shirt and pants on a long-haul flight, for example. With a simple wrap and tie fastening, there are no fussy buttons to deal with.

It is not difficult to knit, but will take a little longer than most of the other patterns in the book.

Which sizes?

To fit ages

3–4	4–5	5–6	years

FINISHED MEASUREMENTS

Around chest

24¾	26¾	29	in
63	68	74	cm

Length from shoulder

22½	24½	26½	in
57	62	67	cm

Sleeve seam

9¾	11	12¼	in
25	28	31	cm

Which yarns?

4 (5: 5) x 50g/1¾oz balls of Rowan *RYC Baby Alpaca DK* in **A** (Thistle 202) and 4 (4: 5) balls in **B** (Southdown 208)

Which needles?

Pair of size 5 (3.75mm) knitting needles
Pair of size 6 (4mm) knitting needles

What extras?

1 button

What gauge?

22 sts and 30 rows to 4in/10cm measured over st st using size 6 (4mm) needles *or size to obtain correct gauge.*

Abbreviations?

See page 125.

Back

Using size 5 (3.75mm) needles and A, cast on 89 (97: 105) sts.

Row 1 (RS) K1, *P1, K1, rep from * to end.

Row 2 P1, *K1, P1, rep from * to end.

These 2 rows form rib.

Work in rib for 4 rows more, ending with RS facing for next row.

Change to size 6 (4mm) needles.

Join in B.

Starting with a K row, work in striped st st and shape side seams as foll:

Using B, work 6 rows.

Row 7 (RS) Using B, K6, skp, K to last 8 sts, K2tog, K6. 87 (95: 103) sts.

Using B, work 3 rows.

Using A, work 8 rows.

Row 19 (RS) Using A, K6, skp, K to last 8 sts, K2tog, K6. 85 (93: 101) sts.

Using A, work 1 row.

These 20 rows form striped st st and start side seam shaping.

Working all side seam decreases as now set, cont in striped st st, dec 1 st at each end of 11th and every foll 12th row until 69 (75: 81) sts rem.

Work 5 rows more, ending with RS facing for next row.

SHAPE ARMHOLES

Keeping stripes correct, bind off 5 (6: 7) sts at beg of next 2 rows. 59 (63: 67) sts.

Next row (RS) K2, skp, K to last 4 sts, K2tog, K2.

Next row Purl.

Rep last 2 rows 3 times more. 51 (55: 59) sts.

Work even until armhole measures 5½ (6: 6¼)in/14 (15: 16)cm, ending with RS facing for next row.

Shape shoulders

Bind off 12 (13: 14) sts at beg of next 2 rows, ending with

RS facing for next row. 27 (29: 31) sts.

Shape back neck border

Change to size 5 (3.75mm) needles.

Break off B and cont using A only.

Work in rib as given for lower edge for 5 rows, ending with **WS** facing for next row.

Bind off in rib (on **WS**).

Left front

Using size 5 (3.75mm) needles and A, cast on 67 (73: 79) sts.

Work in rib as given for Back for 6 rows, ending with RS facing for next row.

Change to size 6 (4mm) needles.

Join in B.

Starting with a K row and working all decreases in same way as given for Back side seam decreases, work in striped st st as given for Back, dec 1 st at each end of 7th and every foll 12th row until 51 (55: 59) sts rem.

Work 4 rows more, ending with **WS** facing for next row.

SHAPE FRONT SLOPE

Keeping stripes correct, bind off 3 (4: 5) sts at beg of next row. 48 (51: 54) sts.

Next row (RS) K to last 3 sts, K2tog, K1.

Working all front slope decreases as set by last row, dec 1 st at front slope edge of 2nd and foll 10 alt rows and at same time dec 1 st at side seam edge of 7th and foll 12th row. 34 (37: 40) sts.

Work 1 row, ending with RS facing for next row.

SHAPE ARMHOLE

Keeping stripes correct, bind off 5 (6: 7) sts at beg and dec 1 st at end of next row. 28 (30: 32) sts.

Work 1 row.

Working all armhole decreases as set by Back, dec 1 st at each end of next and foll 3 alt rows. 20 (22: 24) sts.

Dec 1 st at front slope edge only on 2nd and every foll alt row until 12 (13: 14) sts rem.

Work even until Left Front matches Back to shoulder bind-off, ending with RS facing for next row.

Shape shoulder

Bind off rem 12 (13: 14) sts.

Right front

Work to match Left Front, reversing shapings.

Sleeves

Using size 5 (3.75mm) needles and A, cast on 39 (43: 47) sts.

Work in rib as given for Back for 6 rows, ending with RS facing for next row.

Change to size 6 (4mm) needles.

Join in B.

Starting with a K row and 10 rows using B, work in striped st st as given for Back, shaping sides by inc 1 st at each end of 3rd (5th: 7th) and every foll 6th row until there are 57 (63: 67) sts.

Work even until Sleeve measures 9¾ (11: 12¼)in/25 (28: 31)cm, ending with RS facing for next row.

SHAPE TOP OF SLEEVE

Mark both ends of last row to denote top of sleeve seam.
Work 6 (8: 10) rows more, ending with RS facing for next row.

Next row (RS) K2, skp, K to last 4 sts, K2tog, K2.
Next row Purl.
Rep last 2 rows 3 times more.
Bind off rem 49 (55: 59) sts.

Finishing

Press lightly on **WS** following instructions on yarn label and avoiding ribbing.

FRONT BORDERS (both alike)

With RS facing, using size 5 (3.75mm) needles and A, pick up and knit 77 (85: 93) sts evenly along front opening edge, between cast-on edge and start of front slope shaping.

Starting with row 1, work in rib as given for Back for 5 rows, ending with RS facing for next row.
Bind off in rib.

RIGHT NECK BORDER AND TIE

With RS facing, using size 5 (3.75mm) needles and A, cast on 60 (66: 72) sts, pick up and knit 59 (63: 67) sts evenly up right front slope, from bound-off edge of Front Border to shoulder. 119 (129: 139) sts.

Starting with row 2, work in rib as given for Back for 5 rows, ending with RS facing for next row.
Bind off in rib.

LEFT NECK BORDER AND BUTTONHOLE TAB

With RS facing, using size 5 (3.75mm) needles and A, pick up and knit 59 (63: 67) sts evenly down left front slope, from shoulder to bound-off edge of Front Border, turn and cast on 20 (24: 28) sts. 79 (87: 95) sts.

Starting with row 2, work in rib as given for Back for 2 rows, ending with **WS** facing for next row.

Row 3 (WS) Rib 2, yo (to make a buttonhole), work 2 tog, rib to end.

Work in rib for 2 rows more, ending with RS facing for next row.
Bind off in rib.

LEFT TIE

Using size 5 (3.75mm) needles and A, cast on 61 (67: 73) sts.

Work in rib as given for Back for 5 rows, ending with **WS** facing for next row.
Bind off in rib.

Sew shoulder and Border seams, matching bound-off edges. Matching sleeve markers to top of side seams and center of sleeve bound-off edge to shoulder seams, sew Sleeves into armholes. Sew side and sleeve seams.

Attach one end of Left Tie to left side seam, level with start of front slope shaping. Sew button to inside of right side seam, level with start of front slope shaping.

Stripy chair pad

I really like the colors in this seed stitch chair pad, and think they work equally well for a boy's room or a girl's. If you have the time, it would be nice to knit a couple of similar ones, perhaps varying the stripes a bit, to put on a child's bed. This particular cushion takes a standard 16in (40cm) chair pad, but the stitch is quite stretchy so can probably accommodate a pad the next size up or down if your gauge isn't quite right. For an exact size, though, it usually pays to check your gauge before you start.

The pad has a simple button closing at one end, and it is relatively easy to make the buttonholes (see pages 121 and 122).

How big?
The finished chair pad cover fits a 14½in/37cm square chair pad.

Which yarns?
2 x 50g/1¾oz balls of Rowan *Handknit Cotton* in each of **A** (Celery 309) and **B** (Seafarer 318), and 1 ball in each of **C** (Decadent 314), **D** (Sugar 303), and **E** (Flame 254)

Which needles?
Pair of size 5 (3¾mm) knitting needles

What extras?
5 buttons

What gauge?
20 sts and 32 rows to 4in/10cm measured over seed st using size 5 (3.75mm) needles *or size to obtain correct gauge.*

Abbreviations?
See page 125.

Chair pad cover

Using size 5 (3.75mm) needles and A, cast on 75 sts.

Row 1 (RS) K1, *P1, K1, rep from * to end.

Row 2 As row 1.

These 2 rows form seed st.

Work in seed st for 4 rows more, ending with RS facing for next row.

Row 7 (RS) Seed st 6 sts, *work 2 tog, yo (to make a buttonhole), seed st 13 sts, rep from * 3 times more, work 2 tog, yo (to make 5th buttonhole), seed st 7 sts.

Joining in and breaking off colors as required, work in seed st in stripes as foll:

Rows 8 to 10 Using A.

Rows 11 to 20 Using B.

Rows 21 to 23 Using C.

Rows 24 to 29 Using D.

Rows 30 to 32 Using E.

Rows 33 to 42 Using A.

Rep rows 11 to 42 twice more, then rows 11 to 32 again, ending after 3 rows using E and with RS facing for next row.

Rows 129 to 134 Using D.

Rows 135 to 137 Using C.

Rows 138 to 147 Using B.

Rows 148 to 157 Using A.

Rows 158 to 160 Using E.

Rep rows 129 to 160 twice more, then rows 129 to 156 again, ending after 9 rows using A and with RS facing for next row.

Bind off in seed st.

Finishing

Press lightly following instructions on yarn label.

Fold knitted section in half, so that cast-on and bound-off edges match, then sew side seams. Turn cushion cover RS out and sew on buttons to correspond with buttonholes.

My friend Fred

Here is Fred, who is practically as large as a toddler, but great to drag around, and really easy to dress and undress.

He has a nifty wardrobe, which is quick to knit, too. There are a pair of plain trousers and two simple knitted tops. You can pick and mix between the sweater styles and colors, and the plain thick scarf or the skinny stripy one.

If you like, you could also knit Fred a belt with leftover yarn—why not involve the kids in this and get them to make cord belts using a knitting spool (see page 123)?

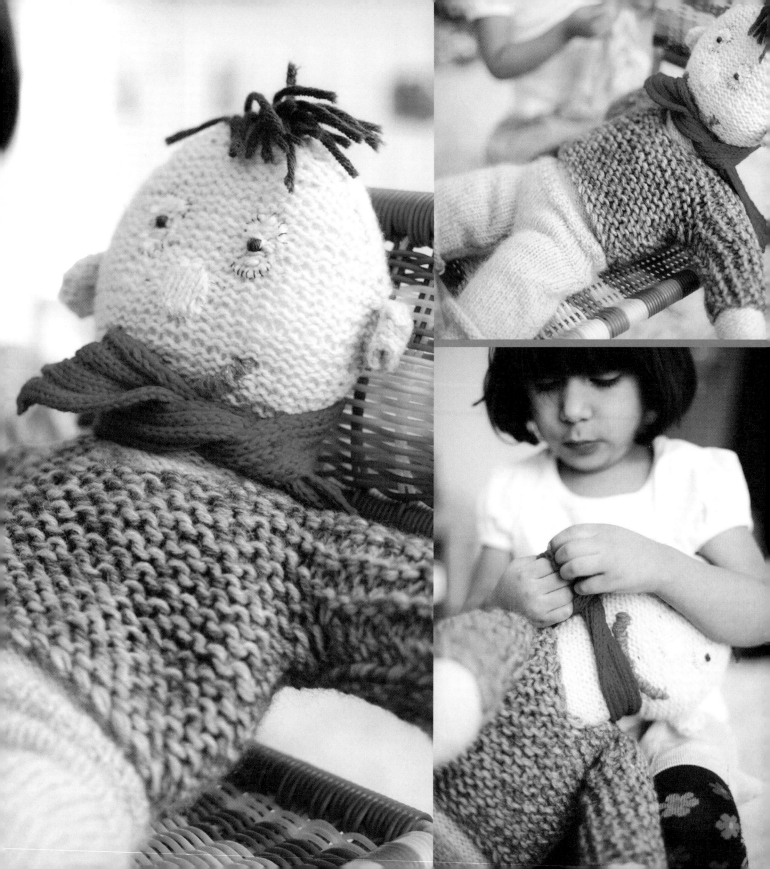

How big?
The finished doll stands approximately 22½in/57cm tall.

Which yarns?
DOLL
3 x 100g/3½oz balls of Rowan *Scottish Tweed DK* in Porridge 024

Scraps of pink, blue, and brown yarn for face and hair
TROUSERS
1 x 50g/1¾oz ball of Rowan *Kid Classic* in Crystal 840
STRIPED SWEATER
1 x 50g/1¾oz ball of Rowan *RYC Cashsoft DK* in each of **A** (Bloom 520), **B** (Lime 509), and **C** (Clementine 510)
MOTTLED SWEATER
1 x 25g/⅞oz ball of Rowan *Scottish Tweed 4 ply* in each of **A** (Storm Grey 004), **B** (Apple 015), and **C** (Sea Green 006)
STRIPED SCARF
1 x 50g/1¾oz ball of Rowan *Kid Classic* in **A** (Sandstone 849)

1 x 25g/⅞oz ball of Rowan *Kidsilk Haze* in **B** (Splendour 579)
RIBBED SCARF
1 x 50g/1¾oz ball of Jaeger *Matchmaker Merino DK* in (Red 231)

Which needles?
DOLL
Pair of size 6 (4mm) knitting needles
TROUSERS
Pair each of size 5 (3.75mm) and size 7 (4.5mm) knitting needles
SWEATERS
Pair of size 11 (8mm) knitting needles
STRIPED SCARF
Pair of size 7 (4.5mm) knitting needles
RIBBED SCARF
Pair of size 6 (4mm) knitting needles

What extras?
DOLL
Washable stuffing

What gauge?
DOLL
22 sts and 30 rows to 4in/10cm measured over st st using size 6 (4mm) needles *or size to obtain correct gauge.*

Abbreviations?
K1 below = K into next st one row below at same time slipping off st above.

See also page 125.

DOLL

Body and head (make 2 pieces)
Using size 6 (4mm) needles, cast on 7 sts.
Starting with a P row, work in rev st st throughout as foll:
Work 1 row.
Inc 1 st at each end of next 2 rows. 11 sts.
Rep last 3 rows 4 times more. 27 sts.
Work 33 rows, ending with RS facing for next row.

SHAPE FOR NECK
Dec 1 st at each end of next and every foll 4th row until
17 sts rem.
Work 5 rows, ending with RS facing for next row.

SHAPE FOR HEAD
Inc 1 st at each end of next and foll 3 alt rows, then on foll
4th row. 27 sts.
Work 11 rows, ending with RS facing for next row.
Dec 1 st at each end of next and foll 3 alt rows, then on foll
5 rows, ending with RS facing for next row.
Bind off rem 9 sts.

Legs (make 2)
Using size 6 (4mm) needles, cast on 32 sts.
Starting with a P row, work in rev st st throughout as foll:
Work 12 rows, ending with RS facing for next row.
Next row (RS) P12, bind off next 8 sts (for top of foot), P to
end. 24 sts.
Work 11 rows, ending with RS facing for next row.
Inc 1 st at each end of next and foll 14th row. 28 sts.
Work 15 rows, ending with RS facing for next row.
Bind off.

Arms (make 2)
FIRST HAND SECTION
Using size 6 (4mm) needles, cast on 3 sts.
Starting with a P row, work in rev st st throughout as foll:

Work 2 rows, ending with RS facing for next row.
Inc 1 st at beg of next and foll 4 alt rows **and at the same time** inc 1 st at end of next and foll 4th row, then on foll alt row. 11 sts.
Work 1 row, ending with RS facing for next row.
Break off yarn and leave sts on a holder.

SECOND HAND SECTION
Using size 6 (4mm) needles, cast on 3 sts.
Starting with a P row, work in rev st st throughout as foll:
Work 2 rows, ending with RS facing for next row.
Inc 1 st at end of next and foll 4 alt rows and at same time inc 1 st at beg of next and foll 4th row, then on foll alt row. 11 sts.
Work 1 row, ending with RS facing for next row.

JOIN SECTIONS
Next row (RS) P 11 sts of Second Hand Section, then P 11 sts of First Hand Section. 22 sts.
Work 33 rows, ending with RS facing for next row.
Bind off.

Ears (make 2)

Using size 6 (4mm) needles, cast on 7 sts.
Starting with a K row, work in st st throughout as foll:
Work 3 rows, ending with **WS** facing for next row.
Dec 1 st at each end of next and foll alt row. 3 sts.
Work 1 row, ending with **WS** facing for next row.
Inc 1 st at each end of next and foll alt row. 7 sts.
Work 2 rows, ending with RS facing for next row.
Bind off.

Nose and eyes

Using size 6 (4mm) needles, cast on 15 sts.
Starting with a K row, work in st st for 18 rows, ending with RS facing for next row.
Bind off.

Finishing

Do NOT press.
Sew Body and Head pieces together around entire outer edge, leaving an opening to insert stuffing. Insert stuffing and sew opening closed.
Sew top foot seam of Leg. Fold Leg in half and sew back of leg and base of foot (cast-on edge) seam, leaving bound-off edge open. Insert stuffing. Sew bound-off edge of Leg to sloping row-end edges of lower part of Body, positioning Leg seam at back.
Fold Arm in half and sew row-end and cast-on edges together, leaving bound-off edge open. Insert stuffing. Sew bound-off edge of Arm to sloping row-end edges of upper (shoulder) part of Body, positioning Arm seam at lower edge.
Fold Ears in half so that cast-on and bound-off edges meet, then sew these edges to side of Head as in photograph.
From Nose and Eye piece, cut out a 1in/2.5cm diameter circle (for Nose) and two ovals approximately ¾in/2cm by 1¼in/3cm (for Eyes). Using photograph as a guide, sew Nose and Eyes onto head—for Nose K side of knitting is RS, and for Eyes, P side is RS.
Using photograph as a guide, embroider face and hair as foll: Using pink yarn, embroider satin stitch mouth. Using blue yarn, embroider satin st eye centers, then work French knot at center using brown yarn. Cut 3–4in/8–10cm lengths of brown yarn and knot to top (bound-off edge) seam of Head to form hair.

TROUSERS

Front and back (both alike)
Using size 5 (3.75mm) needles, cast on 33 sts.
Row 1 (RS) K1, *P1, K1, rep from * to end.

Row 2 P1, *K1, P1, rep from * to end.

These 2 rows form rib.

Work in rib for 5 rows more, inc 1 st at end of last row. 34 sts.

Change to size 7 (4.5mm) needles.

Starting with a P row, work in st st throughout as foll:

Inc 1 st at each end of 4th and 3 foll 4th rows. 42 sts.

Work 1 row, ending with RS facing for next row.

DIVIDE FOR LEGS

Next row (RS) K21 and turn, leaving rem sts on a holder.

Work each leg separately.

Inc 1 st at outer (shaped) edge of 2nd row. 22 sts.

Work 25 rows, ending with RS facing for next row. Bind off.

With RS facing, rejoin yarn to rem sts, K to end.

Complete to match first leg, reversing shapings.

Finishing

Press lightly on **WS** following instructions on yarn label and avoiding ribbing.

Sew side and inside leg seams.

STRIPED SWEATER

Note: Use THREE strands of yarn held together throughout.

Body (worked in one piece, starting at back hem edge)

Using size 11 (8mm) needles and A, cast on 22 sts.

Rows 1 to 4 Using A, knit.

Rows 5 to 8 Using B, knit.

Rows 9 to 12 Using C, knit.

These 12 rows form striped garter st.

Work in striped garter st (K every row) for 12 rows more.

SHAPE FOR SLEEVES

Keeping stripes correct, cast on 12 sts at beg of next 2 rows. 46 sts.

Work 12 rows, ending after 2 rows using A and with RS facing for next row.

DIVIDE FOR NECK

Next row (RS) Using A, K18 and turn, leaving rem sts on a holder.

Work each side separately.

**Using A, work 5 rows, inc 1 st at neck edge on 2nd and 4th of these rows. 20 sts.

Using C, work 4 rows, inc 1 st at neck edge of first and 3rd of these rows. 22 sts.

Using B, work 2 rows, inc 1 st at neck edge of first of these rows and ending with RS facing for next row. 23 sts. Break yarn and leave sts on a holder.**

With RS facing, rejoin A to rem sts, bind off 10 sts, K to end. 18 sts.

Rep from ** to ** once more.

JOIN SECTIONS

Next row (RS) Using B, K 23 sts of first section, then K 23 sts of 2nd section. 46 sts.

Using B, work 1 row.

Using A, work 4 rows.

Last 12 rows form striped garter st for rest of front.

SHAPE FOR SLEEVES

Keeping stripes correct, bind off 12 sts at beg of next 2 rows. 22 sts.

Work 22 rows, ending after 4 rows using A and with RS facing for next row.

Bind off.

Finishing

Do NOT press.

Sew side and underarm sleeve seams.

MOTTLED SWEATER

Work as given for Striped Sweater, using one strand each of A, B, and C held together throughout.

STRIPED SCARF

Using size 7 (4.5mm) needles and A, cast on 9 sts.

Starting with a K row, work in striped st st as foll:

Using A, work 10 rows.

Using B, work 10 rows.

These 20 rows form striped st st.

Work in striped st st for 110 rows more, ending after 10 rows using A. Bind off.

Finishing

Do NOT press.

RIBBED SCARF

Using size 6 (4mm) needles, cast on 16 sts.

Row 1 *K2, P2, rep from * to end.

Rep this row until Scarf measures 19½in/ 50cm.

Bind off in rib.

Finishing

Do NOT press.

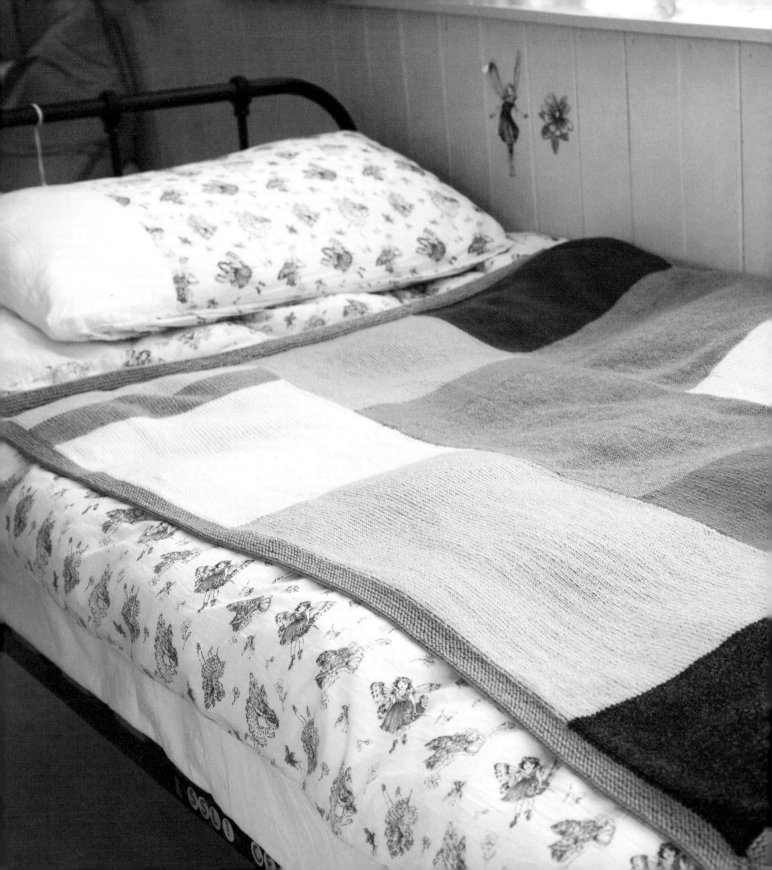

Patchwork throw

This simple patchwork throw, made from blocks of color, with a garter stitch border, will become a much-loved heirloom.

Although it will take a while to knit, it is manageable to take around with you while you knit it, because it is made in three panels, which are then stitched together before you pick up and knit the borders.

You will need to work the borders back and forth in rows on a circular needle because you have to pick up a large number of stitches for this.

How big?

The finished throw measures 37½in/95cm wide and 53in/135cm long.

Which yarns?

3 x 50g/1¾oz balls of Jaeger *Extra Fine Merino DK* in **B** (Smoke 941) and 1 ball in each of **A** (Rose Petal 982), **C** (Coal Dust 978), **D** (Compact 993), and **E** (Ocean 940)

3 x 50g/1¾oz balls of Rowan *RYC Cashsoft DK* in each of **F** (Cream 500) and **G** (Tape 515), 2 balls in **I** (Ballad Blue 508), and 1 ball in each of **H** (Sweet 501) and **J** (Sage 516)

Which needles?

Pair of size 6 (4mm) knitting needles
Size 5 (3.75mm) circular knitting needle

What gauge?

22 sts and 30 rows to 4in/10cm measured over st st using size 6 (4mm) needles *or size to obtain correct gauge.*

Abbreviations?

See page 125.

First panel

Using size 6 (4mm) needles and A, cast on 66 sts.
Starting with a K row, wok in st st in stripes as foll:
Rows 1 to 30 Using A.
Rows 31 to 48 Using B.
Rows 49 to 168 Using F.
Rows 169 to 333 Using G.
Rows 331 to 390 Using C.
Bind off.

Second panel

Using size 6 (4mm) needles and H, cast on 66 sts.
Starting with a K row, work in st st in stripes as foll:
Rows 1 to 96 Using H.
Rows 97 to 114 Using D.
Rows 115 to 246 Using E.
Rows 247 to 390 Using I.
Bind off.

Third panel

Using size 6 (4mm) needles and J, cast on 66 sts.
Starting with a K row, work in st st in stripes as foll:
Rows 1 to 68 Using J.
Rows 69 to 168 Using B.
Rows 169 to 270 Using F.
Rows 271 to 298 Using A.
Rows 299 to 390 Using G.
Bind off.

Finishing

Press lightly following instructions on yarn label.
Using photograph as a guide, sew Panels together along row-end edges, placing Second Panel in center and matching cast-on and bound-off edges.
SIDE BORDERS (both alike)
With RS facing, using size 5 (3.75mm) circular needle and

B, pick up and knit 260 sts evenly along one row-end edge of joined Panels.

Row 1 (WS) Knit.

Row 2 K1, M1, K to last st, M1, K1.

Rep last 2 rows 5 times more. 272 sts.

Row 13 (WS) Knit.

Bind off.

END BORDERS (both alike)

With RS facing, using size 5 (3.75mm) circular needle and B, pick up and knit 192 sts evenly along cast-on edge of joined Panels.

Row 1 (WS) Knit.

Row 2 K1, M1, K to last st, M1, K1.

Rep last 2 rows 5 times more. 204 sts.

Row 13 (WS) Knit.

Bind off.

Work End Border along bound-off edges in same way.

Sew shaped row-end edges of Borders together at corners.

Practical skills

Included here is some useful information that will help you follow the knitting patterns in this book and achieve success with your knits. The pattern abbreviations used are shown on page 125.

Understanding gauge

Correct gauge determines the correct size of a knitted garment. To make sure your knitting is the size you require, you must work to the gauge given at the start of each pattern, as it is the gauge that controls both the shape and size of an article. To check gauge, knit a square in the stitch used in the main part of the pattern. It should be to a size of perhaps 5 to 10 more stitches and 5 to 10 more rows than those given in the gauge note with each pattern. Mark the central 4in/10cm square with pins and count the number or rows and stitches within this area. If you have more stitches and rows than the recommended gauge, try again using thicker needles; if you have fewer stitches and rows, try again using finer needles. Once you have achieved the correct gauge, your garment will be knit to precisely the measurements indicated.

Working to sizes

In a pattern that is written for more than one size, the first figure in the set of figures for different sizes is for the smallest size and the figures for the larger sizes are inside the parentheses. When there is only one set of figures, this applies to all sizes. Be sure to follow the set of figures for your chosen size throughout. (Also, follow either the inch or centimeter measurements throughout.) If 0 (zero) or a – (hyphen) is given for your size, this instruction does not apply to your size.

Achieving a good finish

How you stitch your knitted pattern pieces together is an important element in achieving a smart, professional result. There are two stages to this process. The first is to press the pieces properly to the right size. The second is to stitch them together well and in the right order.

Pressing pattern pieces to size

Spread out each piece of knitting face down to the correct measurements and pin it to a backing cloth—this is called "blocking." Following the instructions on the yarn label, steam press the pieces, avoiding ribbing, garter-stitch areas, and other raised textures such as cables. Take special care to press the edges, as this will make stitching seams both easier and neater. If the fabric must not be pressed, then cover the blocked out knitted fabric with a damp white cotton cloth and leave it to stand to create the desired effect. Darn in all ends neatly along the selvage edge or a color join, as appropriate.

Stitching pieces together

When stitching knitted pieces together, remember to match areas of color and texture very carefully where they meet. Use a seam stitch such as backstitch or mattress stitch (an edge-to-edge stitch which creates an invisible join) for all main knitting seams. Join all ribbing (and neckbands) with mattress stitch, unless otherwise stated.

The pattern instructions specify the joining order of the knitted pieces.

On garments, the shoulder seams are usually joined first, then the sleeves are sewn to the body, so that the center of the sleeve is aligned with the shoulder seam. Join side seams before or after the sleeves are set in, depending on your pattern instructions.

Finally, slip stitch any pocket edgings and linings in place, and sew on buttons to correspond with buttonholes. Lastly, press seams, avoiding ribbing and any areas of garter stitch.

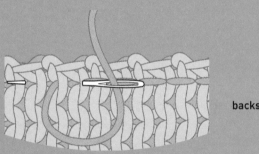

backstitch

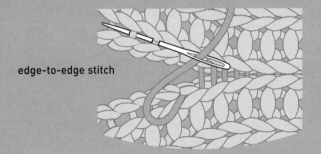

edge-to-edge stitch

Buttonholes

For small buttonholes, a simple yarn-over eyelet is used. For larger buttonholes, you can make horizontal or vertical buttonholes. To knit a horizontal buttonhole, bind off one, two, or three stitches at the buttonhole position. On the next row, cast on the same number of stitches over those bound-off (see below). On the following row, pick up the loose thread at the base of the buttonhole, work the next stitch and pass the picked up stitch over it.

To make a vertical buttonhole, divide the stitches at the

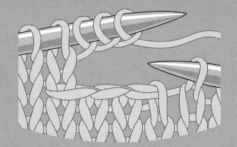

horizontal buttonhole

buttonhole position and work an equal number of rows on each set of stitches (see below), then join up with a row of stitches worked right across both sections.

vertical
buttonhole

Knitting on four needles

Included in this book are some patterns knitted on four needles rather than two. When you want to knit a tube, without a seam, you use four needles rather than two. When you knit, you simply work clockwise around three needles, using the fourth as the working needle. First, of course, you have to cast on the stitches onto three of the four needles.

1 Cast on the required number of stitches (given in the pattern) onto one needle, and then divide these stitches evenly between the three needles.

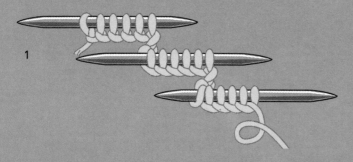

2 To start to knit, arrange the three needles in a triangle. The working yarn will be at the end of the third needle.

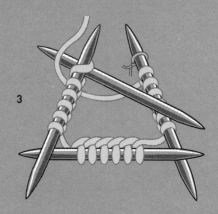

3 Loosely knot a colored thread around the needle next to the working yarn to mark the start of the rounds. Then start to knit with the fourth needle, closing the cast-on triangle when knitting through the first stitch on the first needle.

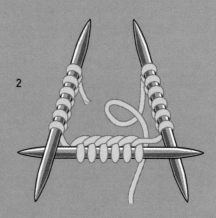

Making cables

These look complicated but are quite easy, and are used in the Denim sweater and scarf on page 64. The twisted and raised pattern is created by slipping a set number of stitches onto a holding needle, called a cable needle (which is a short, double pointed needle), working a similar set number of stitches and then working the stitches held on the cable needle. The cable instructions are written into the pattern using a standard abbreviation, which is explained at the beginning of the instructions on page 66.

Spool knitting

You can buy a knitting spool with four sets of double pins at the top and a hole in the middle (also known as a knitting dolly, as some are made with a doll's face on the spool). It is ideal for making drawstrings and cords, and your children may well enjoy making these cords themselves while you knit the main pattern, so why not get them involved?

It works as follows: to make a knitted cord, drop the tail end of the chosen ball of yarn through the hole in the center of the spool, and wind the ball yarn around each of the pair of pins in turn. Then take the ball yarn across the front of each pin in turn, and, using a knitting needle, slip the yarn on the pin over the new yarn. As you continue to work around the pins in this way, a long tube of stockinette stitches forms in the center of the spool. You can make the cord to your chosen length.

Picking up and knitting stitches

When you pick up and knit along bound-off stitches, for example when picking up stitches at the neck of a garment, it can help to avoid unsightly holes if you knit through both loops rather than just one loop.

When picking up and knitting stitches along the straight edge of the neck (through bound-off stitches), insert the needle through both loops, as shown below.

knitting through both loops

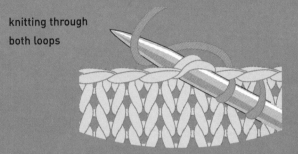

Picking up dropped stitches

If a stitch is accidentally dropped, even if it has unraveled a few rows down, it is easier to use a crochet hook to pick the stitch or stitches up. To pick up knit stitches, insert the hook into the dropped stitch, catch the bar lying above the dropped stitch and pull it through. To pick up purl stitches, simply turn the work over and use the same method as for knit stitches.

Joining in new yarn

Whenever possible, join a new ball of yarn at the beginning of a row. Where a new ball of yarn has to be joined in the middle of a row, you can make a neat join by splicing the yarn. Unravel a short length of the yarn from the old ball and the new one, and cut away a strand or two from each. Twist the remaining strands together to make one thickness of yarn. Knit carefully through this join, trimming off any stray ends.

Templates

FROG TEMPLATE

This is the template for the appliqué frog on the boy's sweater on page 36. It is shown here at 50 percent of actual size, so enlarge it on a photocopier to achieve the right size.

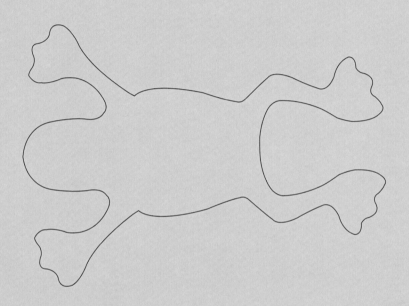

RABBIT TEMPLATE

This is the template for the appliqué rabbit on the girl's sweater on page 36. It is shown here at 50 percent of actual size, so enlarge it on a photocopier to achieve the right size.

Abbreviations

The following abbreviations are used for the patterns in this book. Explanations for special abbreviations are given with the patterns.

alt	alternate
approx	approximately
beg	begin(ning)
CC	contrasting color
cm	centimeter(s)
cont	continu(e)(ing)
dec	decreas(e)(ing)
DK	double knitting (a medium-weight yarn)
foll	follow(s)(ing)
g	gram(s)
in	inch(es)
inc	increas(e)(ing)
K	knit
K2tog	knit next 2 sts together
m	meter(s)
M1	make one st; pick up strand between st just knit and next st with tip of left needle and work into back of it
MC	main color
mm	millimeter(s)
oz	ounce(s)
P	purl
P2tog	purl next 2 sts together
patt	pattern; or work in pattern
psso	pass slipped stitch over
rem	remain(s)(ing)
rep	repeat(s)(ing)

rev st st	reverse stockinette stitch; purl sts on RS rows and knit sts on WS rows
RS	right side
skp	slip 1, knit 1, pass slipped stitch over stitch just knit (one stitch decreased)
sk2p	slip 1, knit 2 together, pass slipped stitch over stitch just knit together (2 stitches decreased)
sl	slip
st(s)	stitch(es)
st st	stockinette stitch; knit sts on RS rows and purl sts on WS rows
tbl	through back of loop(s)
tog	together
WS	wrong side
yo	yarn over

* Repeat instructions after asterisk/s or between asterisk/s as many times as instructed.

[ ] Repeat instructions inside brackets as many times as instructed.

Yarns

The following list covers the yarns used in this book. All the information was correct at the time of publication, but yarn companies change their products frequently and cannot guarantee that the yarn types or shades used will be available when you come to use these patterns.

For the best results, always use the yarn specified in your knitting pattern. The yarn descriptions here will help you find a substitute if necessary. When substituting yarns, always check the gauge and the ball length are similar.

Always check the yarn label for care instructions.

JAEGER BABY MERINO 4 PLY

A lightweight 100 percent merino wool machine-washable yarn; 200yd/183m per 1¾oz/50g ball; 28 sts and 36 rows to 4in/10cm measured over st st using size 3 (3¼mm) needles.

JAEGER EXTRA FINE MERINO DK

An medium-weight wool yarn; 100 percent extra fine merino wool; approx 137yd/125m per 1¾oz/50g ball; 22 sts and 30–32 rows to 4in/10cm measured over st st using size 5–6 (3¾–4mm) needles.

JAEGER MATCHMAKER MERINO DK

A medium-weight 100 percent merino wool machine-washable yarn; 131yd/120m per 1¾oz/50g ball; 22 sts and 30 rows to 4in/10cm measured over st st using size 6 (4mm) needles.

ROWAN BIG WOOL

A heavy weight 100 percent merino wool yarn; 87yd/80m per 3½oz/100g ball; 7½–9 sts and 10–12½ rows to 4in/10cm measured over st st using size 15 or 19 (10mm or 15mm) needles.

ROWAN CALMER

A medium-weight cotton-mix yarn; 75 percent cotton, 25 percent acrylic/microfiber; approx 175yd/160m per 1¾oz/50g ball; 21 sts and 30 rows to 4in/10cm measured over st st using size 8 (5mm) needles.

ROWAN COTTON ROPE

A medium/chunky weight cotton yarn: 55 percent cotton, 45 percent acrylic; approx 63yd/58m per 1¾oz/50g ball; 15 sts and 20 rows to 4in/10cm measured over st st using size 10 (6mm) needles.

ROWAN DENIM

A medium-weight cotton yarn; 100 percent cotton; approx 102yd/93m per 1¾oz/50g ball; 20 sts and 28 rows (before washing) and 20 sts and 32 rows (after washing) to 4in/10cm measured over st st using size 6 (4mm) needles.

ROWAN 4 PLY COTTON

A lightweight cotton yarn; 100 percent cotton; approx 186yd/170m per 1¾oz/50g ball; 27–29 sts and 37–39 rows to 4in/10cm measured over st st using size 2–3 (3–3¼mm) needles.

ROWAN 4 PLY SOFT

A lightweight wool yarn; 100 percent merino wool; approx 191yd/175m per 1¾oz/50g ball; 28 sts and 36 rows to 4in/10cm measured over st st using size 3 (3¼mm) needles.

ROWAN HANDKNIT COTTON

A medium-weight 100 percent cotton yarn; approx 93yd/85m per 1¾oz/50g ball; 19–20 sts and 28 rows to 4in/10cm measured over st st using size 6–7 (4–4.5mm) needles.

ROWAN KID CLASSIC

A medium-weight mohair-mix yarn; 70 percent lambswool, 26 percent kid mohair, 4 percent nylon; approx 153yd/140m per 1¾oz/50g ball; 18–19 sts and 23–25 rows to 4in/10cm measured over st st using size 8–9 (5–5½mm) needles.

ROWAN KIDSILK HAZE

A lightweight mohair-mix yarn; 70 percent super kid mohair, 30 percent silk; approx 229yd/210m per 1oz/25g ball; 18–25 sts and 23–34 rows to 4in/10cm measured over st st using size 3–8 (3¼–5mm) needles.

ROWAN RYC BABY ALPACA DK

A medium-weight 100 percent pure alpaca yarn; approx 109yd/100m per 1¾oz/50g ball; 22 sts and 30 rows to 4in/10cm measured over st st using size 6 (4mm) needles.

ROWAN RYC CASHCOTTON 4 PLY

A lightweight cotton mix yarn; 35 percent cotton, 25 percent polyamide, 18 percent angora, 13 percent viscose, 9 percent cashmere; approx 197yd/180m per 1¾oz/50g ball; 28 sts and 36 rows to 4in/10cm measured over st st using size 3 (3¼mm) needles.

ROWAN RYC CASHSOFT DK

A medium-weight extra fine merino yarn; 33 percent microfiber and 10 percent cashmere; approx 142yd/130m per 1¾oz/50g ball; 28 sts and 36 rows to 4in/10cm measured over st st using size 3 (3¼mm) needles.

ROWAN SCOTTISH TWEED DK

A medium-weight 100 percent pure new wool yarn; approx 123yd/113m per 1¾oz/50g ball; 20–22 sts and 28–30 rows to 4in/10cm measured over st st using size 6 (4mm) needles.

ROWAN SCOTTISH TWEED 4 PLY

A lightweight 100 percent pure new wool yarn; approx 120yd/110m per 1oz/25g ball; 26–28 sts and 38–40 rows to 4in/10cm measured over st st using size 2–3 (3–3¼mm) needles.

ROWAN SCOTTISH TWEED CHUNKY

A heavy-weight 100 percent pure new wool yarn; 109yd/100m per 3½oz/100g ball; 12 sts and 16 rows to 4in/10cm measured over st st using size 11 (8mm) needles.

ROWAN WOOL COTTON

A medium-weight yarn; 50 percent merino wool, 50 percent cotton; approx 123yd/113m per 1¾oz/50g ball; 22–24 sts and 30–32 rows to 4in/10cm measured over st st using size 5–6 (3¼–4mm) needles.

Suppliers

Below is the list of overseas distributors for Rowan and Jaeger handknitting yarns; contact them for suppliers near you/in your country or contact the main office in the UK or the Rowan website for any others.

UK
Rowan Yarns, Green Lane Mill, Holmfirth, West Yorkshire HD9 2DX. Tel: 01484 681881. E-mail: mail@knitrowan.com www.knitrowan.com

AUSTRALIA
Australian Country Spinners, 314 Albert Street, Brunswick, Victoria 3056. Tel: (03) 9380 3888. E-mail: sales@auspinners.com.au

BELGIUM
Pavan, Meerlaanstraat 73, B9860 Balegem (Oosterzele). Tel: (32) 9 221 8594. E-mail: pavan@pandora.be

CANADA
Diamond Yarn, 9697 St Laurent, Montreal, Quebec H3L 2N1. Tel: (514) 388 6188. Diamond Yarn (Toronto), 155 Martin Ross, Unit 3, Toronto, Ontario M3J 2L9. Tel: (416) 736-6111. E-mail: diamond@diamondyarn.com

FINLAND
Coats Opti Oy, Ketjutie 3, 04220 Kerava. Tel: (358) 9 274 871. Fax: (358) 9 2748 7330. E-mail: coatsopti.sales@coats.com

FRANCE
Elle Tricot, 8 Rue du Coq, 67000 Strasbourg. Tel: (33) 3 88 23 03 13. E-mail: elletricot@agat.net www.elletricote.com

GERMANY
Wolle & Design, Wolfshovener Strasse 76, 52428 Julich-Stetternich. Tel: (49) 2461 54735. E-mail: Info@wolleunddesign.de www.wolleunddesign.de Coats GMBH, Eduardstrasse 44, D-73084 Salach. Tel: (49) 7162/14-346. www.coatsgmbh.de

HOLLAND
de Afstap, Oude Leliestraat 12, 1015 AW Amsterdam. Tel: (31) 20 6231445.

HONG KONG
East Unity Co Ltd, Unit B2, 7/F Block B, Kailey Industrial Centre, 12 Fung Yip Street, Chai Wan. Tel: (852) 2869 7110.

ICELAND
Storkurinn, Laugavegi 59, 101 Reykjavik. Tel: (354) 551 8258. E-mail: malin@mmedia.is

ITALY
D.L. srl, Via Piave 24–26, 20016 Pero, Milan. Tel: (39) 02 339 10 180.

JAPAN
Puppy Co Ltd, T151-0051, 3-16-5 Sendagaya, Shibuyaku, Tokyo. Tel: (81) 3 3490 2827. E-mail: info@rowan-jaeger.com

KOREA
Coats Korea Co Ltd, 5F Kuckdong B/D, 935-40 Bangbae-Dong, Seocho-Gu, Seoul. Tel:(82) 2 521 6262. Fax: (82) 2 521 5181.

NORWAY
Coats Knappehuset A/S, Postboks 63, 2801 Gjovik. Tel: (47) 61 18 34 00.

SINGAPORE
Golden Dragon Store, 101 Upper Cross Street #02-51, People's Park Centre, Singapore. Tel: (65) 6 5358454.

SOUTH AFRICA
Arthur Bales PTY, PO Box 44644, Linden 2104. Tel: (27) 11 888 2401.

SPAIN
Oyambre, Pau Claris 145, 80009 Barcelona. Tel: (34) 670 011957. E-mail: comercial@oyambreonline.com

SWEDEN
Wincent, Norrtullsgatan 65, 113 45 Stockholm. Tel: (46) 8 33 70 60. E-mail: wincent@chello.se

TAIWAN
Laiter Wool Knitting Co Ltd, 10-1 313 Lane, Sec 3, Chung Ching North Road, Taipei. Tel: (886) 2 2596 0269. Mon Cher Corporation, 9F No 117 Chung Sun First Road, Kaoshiung. Tel: (886) 7 9711988.

USA
Westminster Fibers Inc, 4 Townsend West, Suite 8, Nashua, NH 03063. Tel: +1 (603) 886-5041/5043. E-mail: rowan@westminsterfibers.com

Author's acknowledgments

My warmest thanks to everyone involved in the production of this book: to the team at Rowan and to Penny for knitting and Sue for pattern writing; and especially to my models Abigail and Jayden, and to Pat, for assisting; to John for photography, Anne for graphics, and Susan for a fun day in the park and constant support; and to Ras and our families in England and Trinidad. *Catherine Tough*